Lead with Truth

The sacrificial nature of juggling instructional, operational, managerial, and collegial goals often leaves school leaders feeling so desperate to resolve conflicts that they lose self, abandoning their core values and forgetting their "why." In this timely and impactful resource, author and professor "Dr. O" draws on her own leadership journey—a journey where she remained true to her beliefs and commitment to serve BIPOC communities, even when that meant choosing the road less traveled—offering nine anchor principles to help guide educational leaders in returning to their core values; communicate and build trusting relationships with staff members, students, and parents; and recognize their self-worth beyond their role on school campuses.

Lead with Truth is an interactive text that invites you to identify learning objectives and reflect on guided questions throughout the chapters, each of which ends in activities geared to help you make personal connections with the content. This engaging resource is for current and aspiring school leaders who aim to make lifelong impacts and transform their practice while remaining true to their own beliefs.

Dr. Qiana O'Leary is Assistant Professor in Educational Administration for the Texas A&M University System.

T0386413

Lead
with Truth

How to Make a Difference in Your School, Your Life, and the Lives of Your Students

Dr. Qiana O'Leary

Routledge
Taylor & Francis Group

NEW YORK AND LONDON

Designed cover image: Getty images

First published 2023
by Routledge
605 Third Avenue, New York, NY 10158

and by Routledge
4 Park Square, Milton Park, Abingdon, Oxon, OX14 4RN

Routledge is an imprint of the Taylor & Francis Group, an informa business

Library of Congress Cataloging-in-Publication Data
Names: O'Leary, Qiana, author.
Title: Lead with truth : how to make a difference in your school, your
    life, and the lives of your students / Qiana O'Leary.
Description: New York, NY : Routledge, 2023. | Series: Eye on education |
    Includes bibliographical references and index.
Identifiers: LCCN 2022031592 | ISBN 9781032351704 (hardback) |
    ISBN 9781032351377 (paperback) | ISBN 9781003325635 (ebook)
Subjects: LCSH: Educational leadership—United States. | School
    administrators—Professional relationships—United States. | School
    management and organization—United States. | Community and
    school—United States.
Classification: LCC LB2805 .O55 2023 | DDC 371.2/011—dc23/
    eng/20220812
LC record available at https://lccn.loc.gov/2022031592

ISBN: 978-1-032-35170-4 (hbk)
ISBN: 978-1-032-35137-7 (pbk)
ISBN: 978-1-003-32563-5 (ebk)

DOI: 10.4324/9781003325635

Typeset in Warnock Pro
by Apex CoVantage, LLC

To My 3 Gems:

To my dad. Thank you for being my rock. I appreciate your wisdom, your love, and your support throughout the years. To my mommy. Thank you for being my biggest fan and teaching me to love myself. Your free spirit will always live in me. To my bonus mom, Mama Donna. Thank you for preparing me to be a woman of dignity, class, and self-worth.

To My Daughter:

You are my greatest gift. Being your mom has helped me defeat the odds and has given me a reason worth living. You are my legacy. Your brilliance sparks fire. Your smile warms any room. Your talent is refreshing. Your spirit is calm. You are my joy.

To My Students and Staff:

If I've had the honor to teach, mentor, or lead you in any capacity, thank you. I thank you for your patience with me. I thank you for trusting me. I thank you for allowing me to share a piece of me with you in this journey called life. I hope that I was able to give you something worth remembering, because you will always be remembered in my heart.

Contents

Meet the Author

▶   **Dr. Qiana** is the CEO, founder, and owner of Minty Educational Services LLC. Dr. Qiana O'Leary serves as an assistant professor in Educational Administration for the Texas A&M University System. Dr. Qiana is an experienced traditional public school and charter school social justice educator. She has served as an ELA teacher, ELA department chair, extracurricular club sponsor, athletic coach, and school administrator for school districts in the states of California and Texas. She received her bachelor's degree from California State University, Bakersfield, her master's from the University of California, Los Angeles (UCLA), and her doctorate degree from the University of Massachusetts, Global, formerly known as Brandman University. Dr. Qiana has been a school administrator at the elementary school level, the middle school level, and the high school level. Most of Dr. Qiana's experience is with urban schools serving black and indigenous communities of color. In her years of service, she has founded two charter schools in Los Angeles, established two educational nonprofit organizations, piloted district-wide equity initiatives, and mentored college-bound minority students. Dr. Qiana currently teaches graduate courses in school administration and educational leadership. In addition to her full-time course load, Dr. Qiana serves as a college prep mentor for high school students in the United Independent School District (Texas) and Antelope Valley Union High School District (California).

Dr. Qiana has a diverse research agenda with interest in education reform, diversity and equity, student-centered coaching, and transformational leadership. A few of her presentations include the following research: College Access for Students of Color, Building Pathways for Women in School Leadership Roles, Critical Analysis of Race in Schools, Certified Leadership, and Inclusive Inquiry-Based Strategies for Inclusive Education.

During her years as a school administrator, Dr. Qiana was identified as a transformational leader who successfully reduced the high school dropout rate by reviewing data of at-risk students in grades TK–12 and by creating systemic resolutions that improved school culture and organizational structures. Those improvements included establishing collaborative goals from all stakeholders, providing effective support systems for the students, and using the progressive learning model for professional development. Dr. Qiana was trusted by organizational leaders to lead the following campus- and district-wide initiatives: state assessments, WASC accreditation, curriculum design and implementation, parent and community engagement, Title I, school safety, AVID, International Baccalaureate, inquiry project-based professional development, restorative justice, equity taskforce, African American parent advisory council, student-centered coaching, reading apprenticeship, and culturally responsive teaching. Before accepting her current role in higher education, Dr. Qiana returned to the classroom in 2020, where she served as a 12th-grade college-prep ELA teacher in Houston, Texas. During that school year, Dr. Qiana was nominated as Teacher of the Year by her peers, as well as mentored two novice high school teachers. Her recent classroom experience during the pandemic shed a new light on the necessities for effective and intentional instructional pedagogy and culturally responsive curriculum design. Dr. Qiana strongly believes that a high-quality education is a solid foundation for young people. She hopes to continue to use her influence to challenge teachers and school administrators to create learning environments that motivate students in searching their inner thoughts and abilities to discover what truly inspires them.

Acknowledgments

There are so many people to thank who pour into my dreams and successes on a regular basis, but for the sake of this project, there are specific folx who helped me get to the finish line. First, I'd like to thank Jesus, my Savior. There were many prayers and worship moments that helped me reflect on offering my most vulnerable self throughout this writing project. I'd like to thank my right-hand girl, my daughter, Kyla. She has supported me and is truly my biggest fan. She wants the best for her mama. I'd also like to thank my editor, Heather, who took a chance on me. Thank you for jumping on board with my vision from the beginning. Finally, I'd like to thank my village of family members, friends, church family members, educational colleagues, and business partners. My inner-circle folx know who you are and that you're forever tattooed on my heart. This one is for us!

Preface

▶ LET'S TALK

A simple conversation. In a perfect world, I would invite groups of principal leaders from all over the nation to participate in a camp-style retreat to share their experiences, their ideas, and to exchange support. Wait! I'm already doing that. I am the proud CEO/owner of Minty Educational Services LLC, and one of our signature services is called the Principal's Retreat. For two days, we invite school leaders from all over America to participate in an exclusive space just for them. During our time of gathering, we connect through bonding activities, self-care practices, relaxation time, planning and professional development, and of course, networking and making new friends in the profession. The experience has truly been a game changer for all who have been able to join the fun. But what about those who can't join the fun? *Lead with Truth* aims to mimic the conversational connections that are shared with my principal peers. As you read, imagine that you're at the retreat, simply talking to a colleague. The information shared in the next few chapters are derived from my personal experiences in school leadership. Some experiences may be relevant, while some experiences may not be applicable to your role, your school, and your community. My hope is that by sharing my stories, and the stories of other principal peers, you're able to learn that you're not in this alone. It's often said that the role of the principal is lonely, and I say it doesn't have to be. I hope that my vulnerability helps you to see that we're connected, even if we haven't greeted each other yet. Different from traditional conversations, you will not have the ability to speak back to me, but you will have the tools that you'll need to sit down and carefully have a deep conversation with the truth that's within you.

▶ WHAT'S INSIDE

Leading with Truth has nine anchor principles. Each section of the book introduces a theoretical lens of the anchor principles.

These principles are coupled with real-life experiences from my years of serving in school leadership, as well as a variety of case studies from other school leaders. Part I is designed to help you rediscover who you are as a person, which will hopefully transfer over to who you are as a leader. More specifically, the intent is to learn how to silence thoughts of worry that over-consume your emotions and your ability to make decisions from the heart. Part II focuses on the significance of ground-ing your leadership practices in research. You will review my research in conversational leadership and learn how exemplary leaders apply the research in their own organizations. Part III aims to provide you with practical resources for developing and sustaining a strong organizational work culture. Sustainability requires strategic and intentional planning to be grounded in truth. Finally, Part IV encourages leaders to recognize your self-worth and the worth of the people you're connected to inside and outside of education.

This book is interactive and invites you to identify learning objectives, reflect on guided questions, and engage in several activities throughout each chapter. Additionally, there are sev-eral sidebar quotes that aim to highlight key concepts. Each chapter concludes with a reflection activity geared to help you make personal connections with the content.

Learning Objectives. The learning objectives are an overview of the knowledge, skills, and concepts readers should be able to demonstrate at the conclusion of each chapter.

Guided Questions. The guided questions are meant to encour-age the reader to reflect on information presented in the chap-ter and develop their own answers.

Sidebar Quotes. The sidebar quotes emphasize an idea or con-cept the author would like the reader to carefully consider.

Activities. The activities in each chapter are used to help the reader put the learning objectives to practice by performing various tasks connected to the content information.

Although this book is written through the lens of school leadership, the nine anchor principles are applicable to all leadership roles within any organizational structure. Let this be your self-care. Make this reading personal. Make this reading count. Make this the moment in your career when you decide to lead with your TRUE and authentic self, because you make the difference!

Part 1
Lead with
True Identity

Introduction: Understanding Your Why

1

Learning Outcomes for This Chapter

After reading this chapter, you should be able to:

1. Identify truth personified.
2. Understand the alternative to truth.
3. Consider the value of your why.

Questions to Reflect upon as You Read This Chapter

1. What is your why?
2. How does your why align with your truth?

One morning on a typical Thursday, I woke up in my usual haste. At the sound of the alarm clock, my day began with a long list of things that I needed to accomplish. With data over-load, my brain was like the multicolored swivel on the computer when it's taking time to think or transition to the next command. That was me. At school, I was Principal O'Leary. At home, I was Mom the Provider, and in the community, I was the Helper. However, that morning when I passed by the mirror and saw the bags under my eyes from another restless night, I had to stop to ask myself, "Who am I?" It was at that moment that I realized that I wasn't walking in truth. I had abandoned my core values to be everything everyone else needed me to be. While leading and developing schools was in alignment with

DOI: 10.4324/9781003325635-2

my purpose of serving underprivileged children, it had completely taken over my life. The truth was that I needed balance. The truth was that I needed to be whole again. It was evident that I needed to learn how to lead with truth. The sad but honest truth is that many of you can relate to my story because you contend with similar challenges. When was the last time you questioned who you are? When was the last time you said no? When was the last time you did something for yourself without guilt or shame? It's time for a change. It's time for a makeover. It's time to get the truth. Get ready! Your best days in leadership are about to come.

▶ WHO IS TRUTH?

According to the Greek philosopher Plato, *truth* is defined as being objective; it is that which our reason, used rightly, apprehends (Vaughn, 1920). Through this understanding, truth typically serves as a pillar for knowledge and justifies the conditions by which we are expected to live. From a religious worldview, truth is a sign of right standing with the customs and principles of a common belief. In traditional schooling, we teach children that truth is a character trait that one is expected to display. For-profit and nonprofit enterprises depend on truth to determine trends, productivity, and customer satisfaction through numerical and anecdotal data collection.

While all these versions of truth are both applicable and necessary for human interconnections, for the purpose of this book, I would like to extend an offer for us to personify truth by acknowledging her presence and giving her life. Leading with truth would then require us to view truth as a companion who accompanies us along our leadership journey.

> **"**What is true for one leader may not be true for another.**"**

When leaders allow truth to speak to them, eat with them, and sleep with them, the two will eventually become one. Differing from Plato's description, truth would then be subjective to a leader's own background, beliefs, culture, and fundamental values. What is true for one leader may not be true for another. Therefore, leading with truth allows the leader to consider their own uniqueness as an asset to an organization instead of conforming to a set of predetermined expectations that may or may not align with their true leadership style. For example, during my first years in education, I worked for a conservative private school. The implicit dress code expectations for female teachers were to dress modestly. This meant that I was expected to abandon wearing "loud" colors on my nails. The truth was that I loved adding color to my nails. The truth was that my nail designs were a pathway I used to connect with the middle school girl students who adored my nail choices. The truth was that wearing colors on my nails boosted my self-esteem because in my adolescent years, I was ashamed of my dark-skinned fingers. However, I complied to the norms because I wanted to be perceived by my school leaders as a team player, even if that had little to do with working in collaboration with others. I'm sure you have a few examples that you can recall when you disguised your truth to meet the expectations of others. I challenge you to embrace this journey as permission to get back to who you really are. In essence, leading with truth allows you to be unapologetically you.

▶ WHAT'S THE ALTERNATIVE?

Many times, when we think of truth, we immediately ascertain that lies or deception is her inherited opponent. While this thinking is applicable in some cases, I have often witnessed it as not being the case for those serving in a leadership position. In fact, the opposite of truth, with most leaders, is fear. I have seen fear grip the thoughts and the actions of leaders, causing them to abandon truth. Fear of job loss, fear of not getting promoted, fear of low student achievement, fear of losing teachers, fear of unhappy parents, etc. are a few topics that cause many sleepless nights for school administrators. This book gives consent for school leaders to break free from the constraints of fear and worry. This happens by being honest to self and resting with truth on your side. I recently had the opportunity to coach a veteran school administrator who struggled with speaking her truth to the district's chief of schools. Through our time together, she rediscovered that her passion for education involved serving on elementary campuses instead of the high school setting, where she was currently placed. She realized that her teachers and staff had been the recipients of her frustrations simply because she wasn't happy to be there. She finally built the courage to embrace truth by communicating to her direct supervisor, who was unaware of her leadership preferences. The following school year, she was reassigned to an elementary school, where she is currently thriving. Like my grandma always told me, *truth will set you free!*

▶ THE MAGNITUDE OF YOUR WHY

Truth magnifies your why. Understanding your why will ground your worth, direct your path, and free your mind. There are millions of inspirational books and motivational YouTube videos on the importance of knowing why you're involved in your current job role. Too many times we're so caught up in the daily functions of life that we forget our why. In other cases, we never knew our why to begin with and continue to drift aimlessly from day to day, month to month, and year to year. So first, ask yourself, How did you become a school leader? Now, before you give your rehearsed answer, I challenge you to allow truth to help you recall your initial considerations for the position. Did you desire more pay? Did your former administrator affirm you as a future leader? Did you want to reach more children? Are you simply desiring to climb the organizational chart? Did the right opportunity present itself? Or was this something you've always desired? While you spend time reflecting on your answer, allow me to share the first time I considered becoming a school leader.

Two words: Joe Clark. For those who aren't familiar with the name, Principal Joe Clark is the lead character in the 1989 movie *Lean On Me*, played by Morgan Freeman. To this day, it is my favorite movie of all time. In the movie, Principal Clark is tasked with leading a school transformation for one of the most toxic schools in the city, Eastside High School. Throughout the movie, we witness the multiple connections Principal Clark makes with students, families, faculty, and community members. Although every encounter is not the most ideal, Principal Clark manages to shift the school climate, empower student agency, self-reflect on his leadership practices, and improve student achievement. For me, this movie left a huge impression on my life. In all honesty, I really didn't know or even pay attention to the principals at my schools before watching the movie. Furthermore, I had no clue that someone who represented my heritage could be the leader of the school. My truth at the tender age of 8 was that I'd one day grow up to become a principal like Principal Joe Clark.

Now, let's be clear. The character of Principal Joe Clark is far from exemplary school leadership. His top-down approach to leadership led to harmful and abusive relationships with various stakeholders. However, I would like to highlight three productive points that greatly influenced "my why" to becoming a school leader. The first productive point is advocacy. I have always considered myself to be an upstander. *Oxford* defines *upstander* as a person who speaks or acts in support of an individual or cause, particularly someone who intervenes on behalf of a person being attacked or bullied. Even as a child, I found myself advocating for my younger siblings in their time of need. As their big sister, I felt it was my role to protect them from things or people they didn't possess the power to fight against. Similarly, I desired to be a school leader who would speak up against policies, practices, and protocols that prohibited marginalized children from thriving. The second productive point from Principal Clark is building relationships with students. The student characters at Eastside High School understood the value in having a school leader who was firm and loving. I, too, desired to establish bonds with students that would affirm their identities, develop their character, and cultivate their respect for others. The last productive point is setting high expectations. Like for Principal Clark, one of my mottos as a school leader is, *maximized potential produces greatness.* I've always witnessed how many GOATs (greatest of all time) needed a coach, a parent, a spouse, etc. to push their maximum so the world could celebrate their gifts. With this lens, I desired to coach and push GOAT teachers, GOAT students, GOAT staff, and GOAT parents to be the absolute best versions of them, first for them and, second, to benefit the collective efforts of the school. The productive points were developed over time. Each time I watched the movie, I was inspired by something that aligned with my career path, which inevitably led me to "my why" for becoming a principal.

▶ WHEN TRUTH AND WHY ALIGN

Two things happen when truth and why align. The first thing that happens is that your actions become driven by your passion. Think of your why as the soul in music. We all know that there are some singers who simply sing. They may have an extensive vocal range. They may be collaboratively talented to harmonize. They may possibly lead songs and effectively sing as solo artists. But then there are singers who don't just sing—they can *sang*. When we hear their vocal artistry, we experience a soul-to-soul encounter with them. They move us. They make us cry. They make us stand up to our feet. In those moments, we don't consider their age, their race, their gender, or their background; we only consider their soul. Why? Singing with soul and singing with passion cause us to ACT.

The second thing that occurs when truth and why align is that it develops your ability to fight to win and to fight to stay alive. Passion work is exhausting. Let me say it again: When you are passionate about leading others and serving others, it can take a toll on your life. The battles will happen. If they haven't already, just wait for them. And when they do, allow truth to help you fight to win and to stay in the game. Truth will remind you of your why in the most discouraging times. Truth will give you the extra strength you need to battle against false accusation, resistance, disrespect, backstabbing, unfair reprimands, promotional rejection, and many other sufferings my principal colleagues and I may attest to experiencing. In the beginning of my career in education, I sadly assumed that everyone was in education for the same reason, which for me was to do what's best for kids. In some schools, I found myself to be like the lead character in the television show *Abbott Elementary*. In each episode, Janine, played by program creator and lead actress Quinta Brunson, spends countless efforts trying to motivate her colleagues and school principal to produce the same passion that she has for teaching children. Unlike Janine, viewers can quickly discover that the other characters do not possess the same "why" as she. This misalignment creates challenges which most often backfires on Janine; however, her truth circles her back to her why, which helps keep her hope alive. Lead with truth to stay encouraged. Lead with truth to stay strong. Lead with truth like there's no other option.

REFERENCE LIST

Vaughn, L. (1920). *Living philosophy*. Oxford University Press.

Principle 2

Understanding Your Heart

Learning Outcomes for This Chapter

After reading this chapter, you should be able to:

1. Define two types of truths.
2. Examine the root of your truths.
3. Consider how you demonstrate love to those you lead.

Questions to Reflect upon as You Read This Chapter

1. What conceptual truths do you need to investigate and possibly reconsider?
2. How do tangible truths restrict your ability to lead with truth and optimism?

The first time I was introduced to myself was the year of 2020. Real talk. I can honestly say that I thought I was certain of myself at the beginning of my teaching career, but outside of that, most of my leadership journey was lived inside of a bubble. I felt trapped. Trapped by society's image of what a black female leader was supposed to portray. Trapped by the expectations of superintendents, executive directors, board of trustees members, and all the stakeholders who vetted me for the various leadership positions I held. Trapped by the assumptions that

DOI: 10.4324/9781003325635-3

attaining my doctorate degree meant that I was an expert in every area of leadership. Worst of all, trapped by who I thought I had to be for everyone else but me. For someone who thrives on out-of-the-box thinking and who gains inspiration from stories of rebellious heroes, my leadership journey was suffocating my happiness. Like an angel in a snow globe, I was a pretty statue with wings but could not fly. Although many people admired what they perceived of me, the truth was starting to get the best me. In other words, it was time to get real with myself.

I'm not sure why it takes many of us so long to get shaken back into reality, but I'm glad it happened for me. Before walking away, I had no intentions of leaving. I wouldn't have even considered it as an option. I honestly believed that I would spend the balance of my educational career as a school principal. You see, I knew I wouldn't accept a position as a director or move higher on the organizational chart, because I couldn't bear the idea of being too far removed from the kids. I love being around children. I didn't stumble into education by default. I simply responded to my calling to care for and nurture the youth. Nothing more, nothing less. Becoming a teacher was the vehicle I chose to love the most precious and valuable humans on earth. For me, transitioning to school leadership was a sacrifice to offer teachers, staff, and parents the necessary tools needed to expand that labor of love. Maintaining a leadership position at the school site level would have been a great honor. As I write and think back on that idea, I can truly see how delusional I may have been. My truth did not align with my reality. I had to get it together, or else, I would have crashed and burned.

> **"**Something had to change. It was now time for a serious heart-to-heart with me, myself, and I.**"**

As a novice leader, I often wondered why the turnover rate for educational leaders was so high. I didn't understand how leaders who claimed they loved children and who claimed they loved teaching could walk away from such a rewarding career. Nine years later, I was very clear on the why and was trying to figure out how I got here. In all honesty, I simply lost a sense of my truths. Instead of being true to myself, I allowed the industry to define me. Something had to change. It was now time for a serious heart-to-heart with me, myself, and I. The moments when I led with truth have been some of the most powerful moments in my life. It is my hope that sharing these powerful moments will inspire you to respark the relationship flame with the truth that dwells within you.

▶ TANGIBLE TRUTH: UNDERSTANDING THE POWER OF SENSORY DATA

For the purposes of leadership growth and leadership development, we will be dealing with two kinds of truths. The first truth is called tangible truth. Simply put, this truth can be discovered through our senses (we can see it, hear it, smell it, taste it, or feel it). Oftentimes, people refer to this as reality. This truth is significant in helping us identify patterns and consistencies so that we can establish control of our day-to-day operations. For example, a tangible truth is that it takes 17 minutes to get to my job by car if I leave my house by a certain time each day. Therefore, I can put routines in place to ensure that I leave by the designated time in order to control the outcomes of my arrival at work. Sometimes there are factors that I cannot control, like traffic accidents, road closures, or inclement weather, that may impact my outcome; however, most of my travel experiences to work should yield the expected results. Unfortunately, many leaders solely operate from this type of truth. Tangible truth creates a certain level of comfort and security once the pre-determined plans are set in stone. The challenge many leaders fail to address is their inability to lead during uncertain times. In the midst of absolute chaos, members in the organization look to their leaders for reassurance and comfort. These are the moments when I've seen leaders completely lose their cool. One thing to do when opposition arises is to always lead with truth.

The year of 2020 rocked the world. For the first time in my entire human existence, we (humanity) lacked total control. COVID-19, commonly referred to as the pandemic, shut down our nation's education system, health-care system, travel protocols, export trading, employment, housing, food distribution, and many, many other functional processes we have relied on as tangible truths. It was the first time when no one had the answer. It was the first time our world leaders struggled to identify quick solutions. It was the first time we witnessed many unbearable challenges within and outside our nation in pure defeat. Many of us lost hope. Many of us lost our confidence. Many of us lost our strength. All simply because we did not have a truth within our reach. One thing that was witnessed most was the decline of authentic leadership. Leaders across multiple industries either threw in the towel and left or pretended to be stable through false claims and misleading communication.

Sadly, most of the leaders at the decision-making table are more inclined to draft a communication plan filled with deceit instead of being honest with the most committed and hard-working individuals in their organizations. This is usually done in fear. For some strange reason, many leaders believe their colleagues can't handle the truth. This is an example of leadership insecurity. Leadership insecurity is a leader's inability to be transparent during the most vulnerable situations. These leaders believe not having a tangible truth makes them unqualified to lead. How crippling is that? These thoughts stink like must. I call them musty meditations. Musty meditations are negative thoughts about flawed practices that are rooted in poor assumptions. What if leaders challenged this thinking with truth? What if leaders walked in genuine transparency? What if leaders admitted when they didn't know the answers? What if leaders walked in the words of Dr. Martin Luther King Jr.: "It's always the right time to do the right thing"? Truth always wins.

I remember my first experience of leading with truth like it was yesterday. By far, it is one of my top ten memories as a school site administrator. To this day, I'm still connected to the members of that dynamic team. Truth kept us connected. The first month of school was under our belt, and our team was already tightly bonded. Our staff worked well together, and their connections with the students were impeccable. The culture on our campus was unique and truly pleasurable.

It was nearing the end of the summer, but it was still extremely hot. We were preparing for "norm day," and things were not going as planned. Norm day is the day when schools tally their enrollment count to predict the school's budget. The tangible truth was that our site had fewer students than the budget allowed. In other words, we were underenrolled. A great majority of a school's budget is determined by the student population. This is referred to as average daily attendance (ADA). The ADA formula is used to determine the number of days a student has been instructed during one academic school year. When this number falls below the predicted outcome, schools are challenged to readjust their budgets quickly to reduce any negative financial impacts at the end of the fiscal year. Typically, staffing positions are the first to be reduced, so I was informed by my director that I would lose two staff members immediately if things didn't change.

With this news, I was advised to withhold the information from my team. As a new leader, I was confused. My gut told me to tell my team. We were tight, and they trusted me. On the flip side, I didn't want to disobey my leaders or break the positive work vibes my team experienced each day on our campus. My leaders strongly believed that my team couldn't handle the information. After much prayer and meditation, I knew what I had to do. I had to lead with truth. Three days later, I called an impromptu staff meeting after work. I often did this, so the team didn't see anything abnormal about the late meeting notice. Like always, we gave shout-outs and appreciations for the good deeds shared among team members. We read data reports and kept each other in the loop about special circumstances concerning our learners. We were a healthy school village, and I wanted to keep it that way. During the meeting, I stayed quiet until it was my turn to share the news. I held up the student enrollment numbers and explained that our budget could not support all staff members on the roster. I explained that I already knew who I would need to release and that I would be meeting with those individuals separately by the end of the week. Before wrapping up the meeting, I asked if anyone had questions, and one courageous teacher asked, "O'Leary, how many more students do we need in order to keep everybody on staff?" I knew the number like I knew my driver's license number, because it had been weighing heavily in my mind for the days leading up to this meeting. I responded, "We are short 150 students, and we would need them fully enrolled within the next three weeks." I proceeded to close the meeting, but what happened next absolutely blew my mind. As I reflect on it now, I think deep down everybody knew who would leave and who would stay, and they were not willing to let anybody go. I moved out of the way and watched my team move tables and chairs, get out sticky notes and maps, and collaboratively devise a plan to get the students we needed for our site. This went on for hours. Around 7:00 p.m., I ordered dinner for the team, and I only chimed in when they had logistical questions that required my assistance. When we finally packed up to go, I asked the counselor to stay behind and walk with me to the parking lot. I asked her if she really thought the team would pull it off, and she simply said, "We'll see." I drove home thinking about what happened and was more inspired to lead than I was when I first started. It was the best feeling ever!

The next three weeks were really hard for the team. I watched them hit the streets to encourage students and families to consider our school as an option. They made brochures and handouts, they gave incentives for our current students to participate in a referral campaign, they made phone calls during lunch breaks, and they even met up to attend community events on the weekends. They were nonstop working around the clock to reach our goal. By the end of week 1, our numbers started to slowly increase. By the end of week two 2, more and more learners were in the enrollment office, completing their applications; however, it still wasn't enough to reach our target. On Monday morning of week 3, I received an email reminder for my district meeting on Thursday. I knew I would have to give my final enrollment count at the meeting, and our current status wasn't enough to cut the mustard. Tuesday after work, I stayed late to catch up on my exhausting email list, and I'm glad that I did. A neighboring school principal reached out to introduce himself and requested to meet with me about a possible collaboration opportunity. The email mentioned that he received our brochure and heard about the great work we were doing in the community. I didn't think much about it at that time and offered to meet on Thursday morning since it was my only open date and time. As I finished my emails and started packing up to go, I looked at a sticky note of our current enrollment numbers. It read, "75 more to go!" I knew the penmanship of the author of the sticky note and immediately fought back tears, because I knew I would have to release her from her position in three days.

Thursday came faster than I expected. I woke up that morning with my game face ready for the district meeting. I wasn't going out without a fight. I was proud of my team, and they deserved my advocacy. As soon as I walked in the office, our school counselor looked puzzled and asked, "What are you doing here? Don't you have a meeting today?" I had completely forgotten about my meeting with the principal at the neighboring school. I ran back to the parking lot and made a dash to the school. Lucky for me, traffic was light, and I arrived on time. I believe the road angels were looking out for me that day.

I'm glad I blocked out two hours for the meeting, because it lasted longer than expected. First, I toured the entire campus. Then I met with students and families until I was finally asked to come to the back to meet with the principal. I quickly shook my attitude for his stalling me out and greeted him with a smile and a firm handshake. He was kind but straight to the point. Our school's brochure was in his hand. He first applauded our school's mission and the impact we were having on the community. He genuinely believed in our work, which was why he wanted to meet me. It felt good to be affirmed, but it felt better when he offered to refer his wait-listed students to our school site. He explained that he was overenrolled and was looking for a strong school program to provide to the families that he did not have the capacity to service. When I asked him approximately how many students were on his waiting list, his response was, "We have about 100 wait-listed families." I felt my knees wobble and had to quickly snap out of it to stay focused. To this day, I'm still in awe that we ended up meeting our enrollment goal and kept the entire team for the full school year. We would not have experienced that outcome if the truth had not been shared. Humans are survivors. We know how to adapt. I learned to never limit other people's tenacity by underestimating what they can or cannot handle.

▶ CONCEPTUAL TRUTH: PERCEPTION IS REAL, AND IT MUST BE CHECKED

The first time I heard someone talk about conceptual truth was in a book written by Bishop I. V. Hilliard titled *Mental Toughness for Success*. It has become one of my favorite books that I have used as a pillar for my leadership practices. Hilliard asserts that our beliefs are established by four elements: *experience, credible people, repetitive information, and environment.*

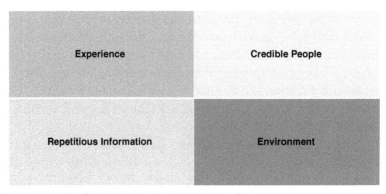

FIGURE 2.1 The four elements that shape our belief system.

What I love most about this theory is that you can use a simple example to grapple with the complexities of this idea. To further explore, let's use a ladder. If you were in the process of hanging Christmas lights around the outside of your house and needed to use a ladder, your belief in the safety of the ladder could be determined based on your personal experience. Perhaps you have used the trusted ladder in the past, which now helps you to believe that you could trust to use it again. "The most potent impact on your belief system is your very own personal experiences" (Hilliard, 1996, p. 68). Perhaps a credible person, like your grandpa, told you to use the ladder. The long history of trust you have established with your grandpa could heavily influence your belief that the ladder is safe. "These authority figures such as our parents, relatives, teachers, and ministers, those whom we are told to respect and listen to, affect how and what we choose to believe about life" (Hilliard, 1996, pp. 67–68). Perhaps repetitious information about the safety of the ladder has developed your ability to trust it. Maybe there's repetitious information shared on a commercial, YouTube video, or Pandora ad that you hear daily and causes you to consider the possibility that the ladder is safe. "Whatever I hear over and over eventually makes its way into my thought process and affects the value system and decision-making process" (Hilliard, 1996, p. 68). Perhaps your environment supports your trust in the ladder. If you grew up seeing people use ladders all the time, or if the ladder was a common tool used in your home, then there may be full confidence that using the ladder will help you accomplish your goals. "What is socially [environmentally] acceptable becomes a part of our decision-making process, and thus a part of our conscience makeup" (Hilliard, 1996, p. 67). The key takeaway is to understand that our beliefs are conceptual truths that we hold deep in our minds. Many times, they cannot be physically proven, but we give value to them based on how they were established in our mind. Conceptual truths are the most difficult to change. As we think about our beliefs as leaders, we should courageously identify their origin and confront their relevance in today's leadership dynamics.

Like many, I was very young during my first teaching assignment. I taught three sections of English to a vibrant group of seventh, eighth, and ninth graders at a K–12 Christian school in Los Angeles County. Although I was new to the classroom, I wasn't new to teaching young people. I actively served as a Sunday school teacher and community leader at various local nonprofit organizations. I knew this was different. I was thrilled to have my first classroom, and I looked forward to pouring into the lives of each kid on my roster.

So many people offered me tons of advice. Advice on how to decorate the classroom. Advice on how to arrange the students' desks. Advice on how to develop my lessons, and advice on which books to read with my learners. Before the first day of school, I had been told many things to consider and many things to avoid. A piece of advice that I was given by a very influential colleague was, "Don't smile until after Thanksgiving." I immediately chuckled when I first heard it, but the look on their face let me know that this was a serious moment of advice sharing. My colleague/adviser explained that my age, my gender, and my race could possibly pose challenges for some students and their parents. They continued to let me know that I must set a firm and strict foundation for my learners so that I could properly manage my classroom. I was so conflicted. My gut instinct knew this was bad information, but I was new and naive and didn't want to make a bad impression with the school administrators. Unfortunately, I drank the Kool-Aid and followed my colleague's advice. I put a plan together, and those kids were in for a rude awakening on the first day of school. There was a new teacher in town, and she wasn't going to tolerate any foolishness.

It only took me three days to embrace the fact that I would rebel against the "no smile" rule. I fell in love with my kids on day one All my classes were extremely diverse, and each child brought their unique personality to our shared learning space. Each day the kids were coming to class and giving me the best version of themselves. It was only fair to give them what I required them to give me. The truth.

One of the first activities of the school year was for each student to bring a treasure chest of items that represented their beliefs, their values, and the very special people in their lives. 100% of my learners presented their treasure chests to the class, and I was delighted to learn and connect with them in an authentic way. Before we transitioned to the next topic, one of my learners asked me to share my treasure chest. It completely threw me off. A conceptual truth in the early stage of my career was that teachers taught and students learned. I hadn't wrapped my mind around the idea that I could learn from the students and that they could teach each other and teach me. I'm so glad that I didn't allow my conceptual truth to become a barrier to this new challenge. The next day, I presented my treasure chest to my learners. We laughed, they asked questions, I told stories, and it even became emotional for me when I showed pictures of my deceased brother. It was so free to be transparent with them. It was so free to be true to them and true to me. To this day, I have been invited to many weddings, baby showers, college graduations, business launch parties, and housewarming parties of the students on my first-year class roster. The bond I share with my former babies has evolved over the years, which has led to a strong legacy of inspiration, courage, and triumph between us. These positive relationships exist today not because I was strict or firm, not because I had great classroom management practices; they simply exist because I led with truth and I chose to smile before Thanksgiving!

What I later discovered was that my colleague/adviser experienced many difficulties with classroom management. As a result, their conceptual truth was that firm and strict teachers yielded better results with managing the behaviors of children. The crippling misfortune was that this person's years of services afforded them the opportunity to mentor many new teachers who worked on our campus. Recycling ineffective practices for new teachers is more common than what we consider. How often do we challenge our beliefs in education? As leaders, are we willing to have crucial conversations with staff members to gain new insight? How may we reflect on determining if our conceptual truths limit our possibilities? As you consider your responses to these questions, you may begin to realize that your practices with leading others may significantly differ from your core values about leadership. More than ever, the current climate in our society invites us to unapologetically reexamine our truths. What people want and what people need are holistic leaders who are completely comfortable in their own skin. To lead change, we must first practice it. Discovering your truth is a process. It requires patience. It requires reflection. It requires listening to others. In the end, however, you will be astonished at how comfortably well others begin to embrace the new and true you.

Recently, I had the privilege to host a few of my former year one students as houseguests. These mature young ladies warmed my heart as they shared their life experiences as college graduates, supervisors, homeowners, dog moms, and wives. To celebrate their accomplishments, we enjoyed a night on the town at several evening venues in the city. They made it a point to let all we encountered know that I was their eighth-grade English teacher. This information always yielded many questions from spectators. During one of these episodes, one of the young ladies began sharing a story about how I saved her life. She explained that one night, she was in a very dark place and decided to run away from her family. Somehow, I caught wind of her situation and contacted several students to get her location. When I arrived on the scene in the wee hours of the morning, I firmly told her to get in the car, where I proceeded to take her back to my apartment for the night. Her parents and my school administration were notified that she was safe and that we'd address everything in the morning. She said that she was so nervous when she saw me arrive and that she didn't know what to expect. All I said to her on the long ride home was, "You're a good kid." When we arrived at my humble abode, I simply handed her a pillow and blanket to crash on my couch until the morning. To be honest, I did not recall the incident, and like the other listeners, I was completely choked up, eyes filled with tears. She concluded her story by telling me, "Ms. O. you were always a real one. We knew we could always trust you to be yourself, and for that, we will always love you." Truly one of the best statements a student can give to their teacher. Truth gave me her honor.

▶ JOURNAL ACTIVITY: NOTE TO SELF

Instructions: Identify at least one conceptual truth you have about either students, teachers, or parents. Try to recall how the belief was established, and determine if the belief is accurate and relevant in your current leadership role.

REFERENCE LIST

Hilliard, I. V. (1996). *Mental toughness for success.* Light Publication.

3

Understanding Your Core Values

Learning Outcomes for This Chapter

After reading this chapter, you should be able to:

1. Identify your core values.
2. Develop a plan to sustain your core values.
3. Establish nonnegotiables/boundaries.

Questions to Reflect upon as You Read This Chapter

1. What are your core values, and how do they show in your leadership role?
2. What is one nonnegotiable/boundary that you will enact tomorrow?

The Truth Trek is the journey or process of learning your true core values. Before we begin the process of discovering your Truth Trek, let me share with you my end results.

I'm starting with the end in mind as the lens through which we'll assess my former leadership practices. I hope that my vulnerability will invite you to learn of my misfortunes as a leader and strengthen you to assess your own. The goal is for the Truth Trek to ignite the true transformation inside of you.

> 66The goal is for the Truth Trek to ignite the true transformation inside of you.99

DOI: 10.4324/9781003325635-4

▶ TRUTH 1: I LOVE BEING AROUND CHILDREN

I am thankful to God for orchestrating my life's purpose to serve young people with eyes to see their value, ears to hear their stories, and a heart to comprehend their truths. My Grandma Josephine wasn't surprised when I declared my profession as a teacher. According to her, I always had it (teaching) in me. After I probed her to explain her rationale, she began to tell me a story about a time in my early childhood. When I started preschool, my mother, eldest brother, and I moved in with my grandma after my parents separated. At that time, my grandma lived in an apartment complex in South Central Los Angeles. My grandma was a nurse, and my mother was a bank manager, so my high school–aged brother watched me most of the time. My grandma had become friends with her neighbor whose son was also a pre-schooler. The two of us played together all the time. His mom says that I was his first real friend. My new buddy was speech-impaired, which caused him to stutter and mumble his words together. At that innocent age, all I knew was that he was my friend who let me boss him around and read to him when we played school. I was always the teacher, and he was always the student. I picked up reading very quickly. By the time I entered kindergarten, I already knew all sight words and was able to read full sentences. I loved reading books. Books were my escape. I didn't fully understand how toxic my childhood was, because I was always reading and pretending to be the characters in the pages. As a result, my literacy and reading acquisition skills naturally developed, and I began to share them with my friend.

Now, each time we played school, I patiently and carefully broke down the phonetic sounds of each syllable when I read books to my play student. We practiced listening and repeat-ing drills routinely, and I also made him practice writing his name neatly in the lines. We had coloring competitions, and we even worked on math skills with my play money set. He was the best student and did everything he was told. He really aimed to make me proud of him. About a year later, our fam-ily moved out of the apartment complex and we lost contact with my friend and his mother. It was a full decade later before I reconnected with my childhood buddy at my uncle's memo-rial service. After the service, we all gathered at my grandma's house to recount some memorable moments in our lives. We were now around 15 years of age, and my childhood friend had developed to be a very handsome and athletic young man. He had charisma and spoke very well. There wasn't a single trace of his speech impairment. To my surprise, he stood up in the middle of the family room and thanked me for teaching him how to speak. His mother giggled and added that his first real teacher was a sassy 4-year-old girl who lived next door, and her name was Qiana. I blushed with embarrassment and found some excuse to quickly get to the kitchen to clean the dishes. I didn't know the seed I planted as a little girl would one day blossom into a prolific profession. Over the years, I was able to recall similar stories of how I helped young children in my community and in my family strengthen their literacy skills. The same love and excitement that I had at age 4 still seeps through my pores whenever I'm connecting with young people. The truth is that they (children) bring out the best in me. After reflecting on many similar stories over the years, I created a simple formula to help me establish meaningful interactions when connecting with children. Loving children requires you to **CAVE** in:

- **C**ommunicate effectively.
- **A**ccept others for who they are.
- **V**ulnerably share your story.
- **E**valuate the relationship often.

Communicate Effectively

When thinking about two-way communication, I immediately think about police officers and dispatch operators. The dispatch operator often initiates communication by informing the police officer of the location and severity of a potential crime. The police officer responds by communicating their current location and their ability to tend to the circumstance. Both parties rely on each other to give accurate information as well as listen carefully to directions that are being presented. They also depend on each other to provide help when help is needed. It is truly a collaborative effort.

Young people require the same systems of communication. Oftentimes, children feel that adults talk at them and not with them, and there is a distinct difference between the two. When someone talks *at* you, they take on the role of being omniscient. They know everything. They know the problem. They know the solution. They know who is right. They know who is wrong. The unfortunate challenge is that we frequently get it wrong with children. Many assumptions that aren't accurate are made about young people. The labels they wear on campus are sometimes inaccurate. As a result, it builds resentment, lack of trust, anger, and fear between children and adults. If you find yourself sometimes struggling to give all children a fair chance, the opportunity for you to start fresh is today. Children are the most forgiving beings. Each day is a new day for you to begin improving your relationship with some of our most vulnerable children.

Have you ever heard a new song for the second time and paid close attention to the lyrics? If you're an eighties kid, then you remember the era of the cassette tape. Young people across the world would spend time rewinding the tape to write down the song lyrics for accuracy. Everyone desired to be the first to learn all the words to sing them at the next party. I call this listening on purpose. Listening on purpose requires you to pause your thoughts and hold your rebuttals. Your goal is to listen to the communicator with accuracy and precision. When appropriate, you recap what you've heard, giving the communicator a chance to correct you as needed. If the conversation is in-person, the attentive listener will observe nonverbal cues to further support an accurate read of the messenger. Nonverbal cues include body language, eye contact, and facial expressions. All these parts of the conversation help make the attentive listening process purposeful.

What systems are in place for attentively listening to our students? Do we use our authority to dismiss their words? Do we help them articulate their thoughts in a nonthreatening environment? Do we respectfully consider them as human beings regardless of their age? Many of us spend many hours designing lessons to help our students think critically about current and historical world events. We train their minds to gather information, examine it, and make conscious decisions. In my experience, I have discovered that students are most expressive when they are passionate about a specific topic, especially topics related to fairness. It's important to listen carefully to our students when put in a position of defense. Most of the time, threatening situations cause students to respond impulsively and irrationally. Identifying a safe space and a safe person to listen attentively can de-escalate conflicts. Furthermore, children who feel heard are more likely to feel valued. Practicing and teaching attentive listening skills will foster a healthy classroom culture and strengthen rapport between teachers and students. After all, everyone deserves the opportunity to be heard.

Accept Others for Who They Are

There is a misconception on the characteristics of a good student. The ideologies of a good student typically don't embody the cultural differences of all students. As a matter of fact, it alienates students who are messy, indecisive, too outspoken, or too shy, who procrastinates, who thinks outside the box, and many other unique qualities that can be identified as unorthodox. Kids don't often feel valued in the school setting. They look to find bonds with others on campus who experience similar challenges or who are willing to accept them for who they are. The irony is that many students with these characteristics grow up to become entrepreneurial trailblazers, like Steve Jobs, or undeniably talented entertainers, like Beyoncé Knowles Carter. It's safe to say that the school is a training ground for the next generation of leaders, and since we don't know who will grow up to do what, it's safe to say that all students are good.

I decided to try this notion out after receiving my Advanced Placement certificate in Language and Composition. My good friend/colleague and I attended training the summer before my sixth year as a high school teacher. My schedule required me to prepare for three sections: (1) Freshmen English, (2) Honors 10, and (3) AP English 11. While excited, I knew this could potentially become a heavy load to carry, especially as a young single mother. I needed to figure out a way to work smarter and not harder. Since I was required to submit my AP English syllabus to College Board prior to the start of school, I decided to model all sections after my most rigorous course. This meant that I was going to raise the bar for my ninth and tenth graders, and I was fully confident my students would meet or exceed my expectations. I knew, of course, that I had to offer grade-appropriate novels, but the strategies and skills taught would be the same. However, I didn't know that the recipe for my successful teaching sauce was in my ability to offer differentiated assessments for the unique learning styles of my students. The student passing rate for that year felt like I woke up one morning and hit the lottery. I discovered that by offering student choice, I had tapped into this concept of student acceptance. Students were able to demonstrate content mastery in ways that best matched their learning styles. Their buy-in yielded high levels of student engagement, which ultimately led to high levels of student achievement. I'm still in contact with many of the students I instructed over the years, and I'm so proud of their successes. Many of them have thanked me for accepting them for who they were as teens while helping them navigate through the many twists and turns of being a high school scholar.

Vulnerably Share Your Story

Relationship vulnerability requires you to let the other person(s) into your thoughts, emotions, feelings, and challenges. Early in my teaching career, I learned how to be vulnerable through telling stories. By telling stories, I was able to connect with others. This has been evident in my role as teacher and school administrator. When people feel connected to me and see that we share similarities, they are most likely to trust me. My stories are true and authentic. Some are humorous, and some are sad, but overall, they are told to help inspire change, reflection, and action.

In high school, my favorite teacher told stories in class. I was captivated by her ability to connect her life's experiences with the characters in the many novels we read in class. She kept us engaged, but most importantly, she helped us realize that she was a real human with real human dilemmas like us. This made her approachable and caused us to trust her throughout our teenage developmental years. To other teachers, she may have been perceived as immature, or maybe even unprofessional, but for us, she was special. Her genuineness had us wrapped around her finger. We were never late to her class, and we worked hard to please her by completing all her assignments. She celebrated us, she mentored us, and she protected us. I didn't know how much of an impact she had on my life. English has always been my favorite subject, but I never thought I would declare English as my major in college. Once I decided I wanted to be a teacher, I knew I was going to be a storyteller, like my favorite high school teacher. Furthermore, I didn't know that once I'd become a mommy, I would name my daughter after her. Vulnerability goes a long way, so share your story. Shout-out to Ms. Kyla Ruben-Watson!

Evaluate the Relationship Often

Can you imagine what would happen if we never attended annual health-care checkups with our physicians? Or what negative consequences we would experience if we spent a lifetime without visiting the dentist? We understand that these routine visits give us an evaluation of the state of our bodies. As children, we are taught the benefits of frequently evaluating our physical well-being so that we can adjust our lifestyle as needed. In like manner, the same requirements are essential for examining relationships. Routine check-ins will help members of the relationship adjust as needed to sustain healthy interactions. The negative consequences for neglecting to pursue relationship evaluations can lead to turmoil in our emotional, mental, and even physical well-being.

The first year I asked my freshman high school students to complete a survey about my teaching practices was a complete game changer in my career. I realized that my class was one of their first experiences as a high school student, and I wanted to get their feedback to learn if I was meeting their expectations as a trusted adult in their lives. Some of my learners were very vocal, so I had an idea of how they felt about me and the class, but some of my introverted students gave very little evidence of their perception about our time together. The survey tool included questions about the curriculum, my teaching style, and the class culture. I was very shocked by some of the information I gathered from all six classes. A large majority of students felt personally connected with me but felt as though the content lacked interest or relevance. The only reason they completed the assignments was that they respected me. While I was happy to have earned their respect, I genuinely wanted them to enjoy my course. I decided to gather a task force of students from my classes. The goal of the task force was simple. I provided lunch, and they gave me advice on my upcoming units of study. (*This is called a culturally responsive curriculum design.*) It morphed into something so magical. The kids felt so empowered to be a part of the decisions regarding their learning. (*This is called student agency.*) They took it seriously, and they held their classmates accountable. I used them as student leaders, and it bridged relationships between students in different class sections. At the end of the year, 100% of the students reported they were happy with their learning experience in my class. The initial check-in was more than a survey, and it provided more than just feedback. It revolutionized the relationships that were created between 120 students and their high school English teacher.

▶ TRUTH 2: I LOVE SERVING PEOPLE

My mama suffered a ten-year drug addiction. During her recovery, a sweet elderly lady donated many beautiful clothes, shoes, and accessories to the rehabilitation center where Mama was learning how to prioritize her sobriety lifestyle. My mama had an eye for fashion. She could design, sew, and create any wardrobe style she viewed inside of her many fashion magazines. Mama made the most of her new threads and happily interviewed and landed her first job post-addiction. She was so proud of herself. The entire family was proud. It was this moment that led to her many years of service to others. She never forgot her humble beginnings and vowed to God almighty to raise her children to become children with a servant's heart.

Being a servant leader is a responsibility. Tarallo (2018) asserts that servant leaders are "serving instead of commanding, showing humility instead of brandishing authority, and always looking to enhance the development of their staff members in ways that unlock potential, creativity and sense of purpose." You are responsible for leading others towards achieving a common mission. You are responsible for establishing a culture of collaboration and mutual respect. You are responsible for establishing and maintaining positive outcomes. Over the years, I've learned the responsibilities of a leader are better accomplished once the leader understands their role as a servant leader. It may sound clichéd, but it's not. Think about it like this: A car driver expects the car to accelerate when they push on the gas, stop mobility when they hit the brakes, give heat during cold temperatures, blast their favorite music jam when they turn up volume. Yet the driver understands these daily functions can only be optimized when proper maintenance is performed on their vehicle. After all, you won't get very far without any gas in the tank. In like manner, a leader drives the team. They push and pull demands all the time. They expect strategic plans to be developed and executed with fidelity. They expect excellent performance and very rarely handle failure well. With all these expectations, it's only right to ensure that the team is receiving proper care. Leading with truth requires leaders to take a step back and ask themselves, "Do I genuinely serve the needs of my team?" Beyond pondering the thought, a great leader takes accountability by seeking the truth from their members.

I've always wanted to make my mama proud. I never wanted her to feel that her sufferings and setbacks were in vain. I wanted her to be proud of her legacy by watching me live out the values she instilled in her children. One of the things she valued most was meeting the needs of others. If someone was hungry, she fed them. If someone needed clothes, she either bought it or made it for them. She has sheltered family members who needed temporary housing. And above all, she always offered to pray for others or at least comfort their hearts with her beautiful singing. My mama was a true gem. I decided to practice these core values as a school leader. My desire was to be a visible and value-added leader that heard the people and served the people. I hoped to uplift staff members, students, and parents by empowering them to use their voice to give insight to my leadership decisions. I knew that I wasn't perfect. I accepted that I was a flawed person, like everyone else I encountered. My position as leader did not exempt me from being human. My mantra was to use my platform as an opportunity to lead a learning space that gave energy and encouragement to all who joined our community. First, I created leadership teams and trained them on how to serve. It was important that all leaders shared the same humility as servant leaders. Next, we created advisory groups that gave all stakeholder members a chance to contribute to small things, like bell schedules, as well as big things, like hiring and budgets. I knew that buy-in was important and creating shared responsibility was the best way to receive it. Finally, I created and communicated my personal leadership development goals. I solicited feedback from the team to help me monitor and pivot my actions. The best service is intentional service. My aim was to demonstrate a genuine attempt to listen, receive, and respond. Like Mama, it was in these moments that I learned the truth about myself. Serving others isn't an option. It's a necessity.

The Lie: Leaders Can't Show Genuine Love to the Staff

The first definition of *love* that I learned was written in the Bible by the apostle Paul. In the book of Corinthians, Paul writes:

> **Love** is patient and kind; **love** is not envious or boastful or arrogant or rude.
> It does not insist on its own way; it is not irritable or resentful;
> it does not rejoice in wrongdoing but rejoices in the truth. . . .
> **Love** never ends.
> (1 Cor. 13:4–8a)

What fascinates me most about this description of love is the author. Paul scribes his interpretation of love after serving as a stone-cold murderer. Talk about a change in occupation! He went from taking lives to appreciating them. From hurting people to helping them. From wiping out a nation to witnessing to a generation. Even if you don't subscribe to Christian theology, it's intriguing to learn of his shift or change of heart towards all people. While I don't consider myself to be an apostle, I did come to realize that I needed to shift my approach to leading others. I wanted to lead and love. It's who I am. In fact, my initial role as school leader ironically was the least time where I exhibited or experienced love. Early in my administrative career, I began to be disturbed by the hypocrisy that educators displayed towards each other while simultaneously shaping the character of future generations. I observed how campus after campus, staff after staff, community after community operated daily without the presence of genuine love. I wanted that to change, so I started with me. I became the change I wanted to see.

I first questioned why it was taboo to lead and love. I wondered if leaders experienced tangible truths with poor results from mixing the two or if leaders held on to conceptual truths that they inherited from others. I decided to do some digging. I wanted to get to the bottom of what prevented leaders from displaying love to their members. The way I did this was simple. I shared stories about different moments when I prioritized people over school policy. Then I would listen to their responses and opinions of the matter. I'm going to share two stories with you, followed by some questions. This is a time for honest reflection, so record immediate reactions. Then go back and think about your thoughts. Question where those thoughts originated, and examine if you're willing to change your approach. Remember, there are no right or wrong answers.

Story #1: The Pregnant Teacher

One afternoon, after lunch ended, a teacher walked into my office with a troubled look on her face. She was pregnant at that time, so naturally my Spidey senses went up as I began to question what was wrong with her. She communicated that she had been to the restroom several times and that she was highly concerned about her body. Much of what she described sounded like she was possibly having a miscarriage, and that was when my love actions stepped into high gear. My thoughts were: (1) We work in the hood. It will take the paramedic too long to arrive. (2) She moved from the East Coast to the West Coast and doesn't have any family except her husband. (3) She is trusting me to help her. Simultaneously, while these thoughts are swirling in my head, my actions were: (1) Brief my assistant principal on the situation and direct her to take over the campus in my absence. (2) Request my administrative assistant to contact the teacher's husband and send him the address to the hospital. (3) Safely escort the young teacher to my car and drive her to the emergency room.

We left for the hospital right around rush-hour traffic. If you know anything about the 405 freeway in Los Angeles, then you know what a nightmare it could be during the peak hours of 2:00 p.m.–6:00 p.m. I knew I had to keep her calm and get there quickly. While there weren't any immediate signs of alarming concerns, I didn't want to take any chances. We arrived safely and checked her in to see a physician. We were informed they would see her quickly, given her condition. She looked at me with tears in her eyes, thanked me for the ride, and said that since she knew I was a busy woman, it was okay for me to leave since her husband was on the way. My response was, "Listen here, I ain't going nowhere until your husband shows up. Whatever is on my schedule can wait. You are my top priority right now." They called her name, and she went to the back to see the doctor. I told her I would wait and direct her husband to her once he arrived. Moments later, her husband rushed in looking distraught and concerned. I could tell that he really loved his wife. I approached him and gave him a brief update. Then I asked the receptionist to allow the young man to join his wife in the back. On his way to the back room, he stopped and came back to me. He placed his hand on my shoulder and gripped my hand and said, "Thank you so, so much." At that moment, I was highly confident in my choice as her school principal. I was also okay with any negative consequences I would receive from our district's headquarters. I was true to self. I led with love, and I was at peace.

ACTIVITY #1
READ > THINK > RESPOND > REFLECT

Instructions: *Now that you've read the first story, think about what you would have done in this situation. Respond honestly to the following questions. Then reflect on what has impacted you to think and respond the way you did and if it helps or hinders your ability to love staff members.*

Do you trust your leadership staff to lead the organization in your absence?	Are you comfortable with transporting staff members in your personal vehicle during emergencies?	Are you flexible enough to dismiss tasks/meetings on your schedule to address unexpected challenges?

Story #2: The Love Plant

One of our instructional coordinators remarried in her golden years. I was fortunate to spend time with her and her husband at a dinner party we were invited to attend. The newlyweds and I had a lovely time, and I was genuinely moved by their love story. On one occasion, my administrative assistant called to inform me that our instructional coordinator needed to speak with me at once. As a school leader, I have always offered an open-door policy for staff and parents. I opened the door and was greeted by her red cheeks and watery eyes as she grieved the loss of her husband's mother. Although we were in a rat race to meet a hard deadline for a big grant opportunity, my love action went into gear to dismiss her to console her husband. I also encouraged her to take time off to support his grievance and not to focus on the grant. After she left campus, I asked our administrative assistant to forward me her address. I sent a simple plant and wind chimes to her husband to offer my sincerest condolences. The couple was surprised by the gesture and was extremely grateful to receive my token of love.

A year later, I relocated 74 miles south from my previous school site. I applied for a principal position and was selected as a finalist for the job. During the interview process, I was required to speak to staff members about my vision for the school and share my philosophy of education. I concluded my presentation with a question-and-answer segment for teachers to learn more about me. One of the rookie teachers asked me probing questions about my previous job assignment. After a series of questions, he connected the dots to discover that I once worked with his mother, the instructional coordinator! I was offered the job. Later that year, I was informed that when I left the room during my interview, the rookie teacher phoned his parents and placed them on speaker for his colleagues to hear their responses to questions about me. I'm not certain about what was specifically stated, but it certainly influenced the teachers and district personnel in the room to vote for me to be their next school leader.

ACTIVITY #2
READ > THINK > RESPOND > REFLECT

Instructions: *Now that you've read the second story, think about what you would have done in this situation. Respond honestly to the following questions. Then reflect on what has impacted you to think and respond the way you did and if it helps or hinders your ability to love staff members.*

Do you have an open-door policy for staff to connect with you at any time?	How do you support staff dealing with a family loss? Do you offer them extended time to grieve?	Would you have dismissed an important team member from meeting a high-priority deadline so they could address a personal matter?

Leading with truth requires you to uncover your core values. You must unpack what makes you uniquely you. When you do this, you position yourself to have clarity on prioritizing the things that matter most to you. I like to call these my nonnegotiables/boundaries. These are the values that I will not compromise on regardless of the money offered or new policies enacted. To help you begin the journey of discovering your true nonnegotiables, I have created a process called the Truth Trek. Please see the example in the following map to guide you through successfully completing the activity.

ACTIVITY #3
THE TRUTH TREK

Follow the following steps to help you determine your leadership core values.

Step 1: List three of the happiest moments in your life.
Step 2: List three things that deeply trouble your heart.
Step 3: List three of your personal or professional gifts and talents.
Step 4: Identify a single word or phrase that summarizes your lists in steps 1–3.
Step 5: Create three core values statements that will anchor your leadership decisions.

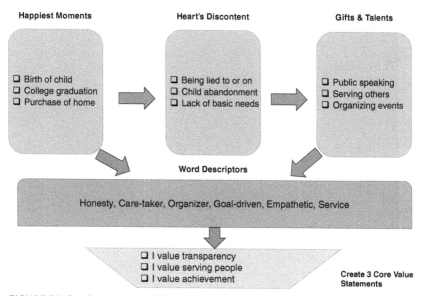

FIGURE 3.1 Graphic organizer of the Truth Trek.

▶ JOURNAL ACTIVITY: NOTE TO SELF

Instructions: Write a letter to yourself identifying your core values and your plan on incorporating them into your leadership decisions. Read your letter aloud to yourself one year from today's date.

REFERENCE LIST

Tarallo, M. (2018). The art of servant leadership. *Security Management Magazine.* www.shrm.org/resourcesandtools/hr-topics/organizational-and-employee-development/pages/the-art-of-servant-leadership.aspx

Part 2
Lead with True Research

Principle 4

Understanding Your Audience

Learning Outcomes for This Chapter

After reading this chapter, you should be able to:

1. Identify generational characteristics in the workforce.
2. Consider how your professional preferences differ/ align with the preferences of those you lead.
3. Listen to learn about what matter to those you lead.

Questions to Reflect upon as You Read This Chapter

1. What is your communication style?
2. How do you consider the communication styles of others?

During a routine district school administrator's meeting, 50 administrators were asked to complete a survey regarding the most essential characteristics required for a great school leader. The list consisted of five simple traits, and each of us was asked to rank them in order of necessity, with number 1 representing the most important trait and number 5 representing the least important trait. Following the survey, we were asked to share our information with the colleagues sitting at our table. Once we completed the small-group discussion, we were asked to share our outcomes with the whole group. I recall looking at the list

DOI: 10.4324/9781003325635-6

and being able to instantly identify my number 1 trait: under-standing people! It didn't take me much longer to quickly rank the other traits, because I felt each of the others did not have any special priority over the other. These five minutes seemed like an eternity for the colleagues around me as I watched them toil, sweat, and contemplate their responses to the survey assign-ment. A spider on the wall could have assumed their survey response was the determining factor of a promotion, as many squirmed anxiously in their seats. Saved by the bell—it was now time for us to share our information at our table group.

Immediately, my principal shared his answers in a matter-of-fact tone. He carefully communicated the justifications for his choices and concluded his response by reminding each of us of his years of service as a school administrator. One by one, each person at my table shared their responses, and each of them had well-thought-out evidence to support their claim. I was last to share my results, and for a moment, a feeling of intimidation tried to consume my thoughts. For starters, I was the only black female administrator in the room, and I was one of the youngest administrators in the district. None of the others had selected my choice as their number 1 trait, and I was beginning to ques-tion my own choice. It was at that split moment that I had to remind myself of the advice I had shared with my students over the years: "The truth is in your belly, so trust your gut." Based on my experiences as an educator, a mother, a sibling, a neigh-bor, a student, etc., my successes with others were based on my ability to understand them and respect their perspectives. Their perspectives were their truths, even if they differed from mine. At the end of the small-group discussion, the superintendent of schools divided us into five groups based on our number 1 sur-vey trait. Only one other person joined me in our group trait. Like me, she shared a strong passion for desiring to connect to and understand all members of the school community. The superintendent walked to each group and announced the attri-butes and future positions people in each group would most likely rank on our organizational chart. Our group was last, which gave me a couple of minutes to render a silent prayer to God in hopes that we would not undergo public humilia-tion. According to his descriptions, each of the previous groups appeared to have all the successes. When he finally approached our group, he hesitated for a moment and began to state how shocked he was to see so few participants. He stared at my colleague and me for a long, hard time and then looked back at the audience and requested that they, too, take a long, hard stare at us, because we would be the district's future superintendents.

I drove home thinking deeply about the meeting. I wasn't so much concerned about what our superintendent stated, although I was really flattered. Instead, I spent most of my drive thinking about when and how I began to understand people. Although I attended a great graduate school, I did not learn how to understand people in my master's courses. Although I had a great rapport with students and their families as a classroom teacher, I believe I had already acquired the trait long before I stepped inside the classroom. Then it dawned on me. I really began to understand people and their emotions from first learning how to effectively communicate with my own family and in my own community. I was raised with six brothers and one sister, so learning about my siblings was my first encounter with understanding others who think and act differently. We were taught how to share, how to respect each other's privacy, how to celebrate each other's accomplishments, how to hold one another accountable to our goals, how to disagree with taste, and how to help each other when needed. Loving each other was not debatable with our parents; it was required. Think about the people in your family whom you grew up with and how you communicate with each other. How have those encounters impacted your approach to communicating with others?

Communication is the key component to connecting with those you lead. Let's face it. The most toxic work environments lack (1) a general sense of vision and structure, (2) respect and transparency, or (3) proper communication. And while the first two are essential in making the workplace transcend from good to great, creating better communication opportunities to discuss organizational barriers could potentially give folks the desire to stay and work through the weeds or give them the freedom to leave.

With a minor in communication, I have found myself intrigued with understanding the power dynamics connected to healthy conversations. In fact, I wrote an entire dissertation on Groysberg and Slind's conversational leadership framework. I'm going to share my findings with you in just a moment, but before I take a deep dive into a theoretical lens, I want you to first explore your work dynamics by completing a simple exercise about your colleagues. Grab a sticky pad and jot down the names of folks in your department or who work closely with you on special group projects. Be sure to use one sticky note for each person. Next, I want you to group them by generation. The first group will be labeled *Baby Boomers*. Do your best estimate on age and place persons aged 58 to 76 in this group. The next group will be *Generation X*. Place persons aged 42 to 57 in this group. The last group will be *Generation Y* (millennials). Place persons aged 22 to 41 in this group. Depending on the workspace, you may have a few folks in Generation Z, but for this exercise we will exclude them. Now, once you have your data collected, I invite you to read some general information about each generation that I discovered during my research studies. This information will serve as the basis to help us unpack the truth about our conversations for Principle 5.

ACTIVITY #4
KNOW YOUR AUDIENCE TALLY

Guess the ages of your campus colleagues.
Group them according to the generations listed in the following.

Baby Boomers	Generation X	Millennials
Ages: 57–75	Ages: 41–56	Ages: 25–40
Total:	**Total:**	**Total:**

Baby boomers. The largest generational cohort in the US workplace consists of individuals born between 1946 and 1964, known for high education levels, dual-income households, the need for individuality, and a focus on health (Loroz & Helgeson, 2013; Marcinkus Murphy, 2012). In the workplace, boomers prefer independence and will challenge authority (Langdon, 2012). Additionally, boomers believe they have the ability to make a difference in the world (Meredith et al., 2002).

Generation X. The generational cohort following the baby boomers, consisting of individuals born between 1965 and 1980, characterized as an independent generation that started the push for a better work-life balance (Krahn & Galambos, 2014). In the workplace, the Gen X cohort has no reservations with questioning and prefers environments where information sharing is prevalent (Langdon, 2012). They consider themselves resourceful and independent, and they value the opinion of leadership (Lancaster & Stillman, 2002; Meredith et al., 2002).

Millennials. An emerging generational cohort of individuals born between 1981 and 2000, characterized as digital natives who want personalized work experiences, place a high value on a work-life balance, and want to have their voices heard so they can make an impact (Kappel, 2012; Marcinkus Murphy, 2012). In the workplace, millennials appear to be authority-driven, and they will rebel against unjust and unfair programmatic processes (Lancaster & Stillman, 2002). They tend to be more concerned with their peer groups and will stand firm on their beliefs (Langdon, 2012). Similar to baby boomers, millennials believe they have the ability to make a difference in the world (Meredith et al., 2002).

At different points in the organizational structure, generations communicate with coworkers (Langdon, 2012). Newer organizational structures and intercommunication processes will drive the generational cohorts to interact on a more frequent basis (Schultz, 2010). The generations that are currently in the workforce have differing views on communication and the media by which communication should be conveyed (Burmeister, 2008; Gibson, 2009), and leaders must understand these differences to sustain a positive and productive work climate (Yost, 2013). Sherman (2006) suggested that leaders must have the capability of using different methods and mediums to better address generational cohort differences. Lines (2004) claimed that organizations that include their workforce in change initiative decisions are less likely to meet resistance, and the leader's role is to find the most effective method to communicate clearly and concisely his or her intentions (Langdon, 2012). Understanding the preferred methods of communication to the three predominant generational cohorts will assist in creating transparency, underpinning the success of change initiatives (Sherman, 2006).

▶ WHAT DOES IT ALL MEAN?

A recurring theme in organizational research is generational differences in the workplace (Yost, 2013). Communication barriers in multigenerational work environments are a major concern for organizational leaders. Managing multiple generations can be difficult (Bourne, 2009).

> 66 Staff members must feel seen and must possess the ability to be heard even when they are silent. 99

Generations are distinctively defined by common beliefs and norms and are shaped by the important and historical events that dictate society during influential adolescence and young adult years (Arsenault, 2004; McNamara, 2005). These differences are factors that contribute to the unique qualities that are infused into a single workplace by the three distinct generations of employees which we just reviewed. Many leaders serve in multigenerational organizations, but their leadership style only speaks to a particular group of people. Lack of this awareness could damage the leader's ability to create and sustain healthy work relationships, which ultimately results in low employee retention. Staff members must feel seen and must possess the ability to be heard even when they are silent. Leading with truth requires leaders to self-reflect and assess how well they know the people who work hard to support them. The sooner, the better. For some leaders, this may appear to be too "touchy-feely," and for others they can't imagine when they would have the time to think about it. As for me, vision became clearer, work became lighter, and people were happier once I finally decided to pay attention and listen to how my staff felt about me as their leader. This, my friends, was my true epiphany of "keeping it real."

▶ THE LISTENING TOUR

Communication serves as the foundation to the daily operation, effectiveness, and competitive advantage of an organization by fostering significant context about the organization's mission, vision, goals, and strategy (Anjaiah & Sekhar, 1995; Edstrom & Galbraith, 1977). Goldhaber (1974) defined *organizational communication* as the "flow of messages within a network of interdependent relationships" (p. 108). Brownell and Lundberg (1993) defined *organizational communication* as the patterned process of sharing meaningful information among social entities or members with roles in an organization. Redding and Tompkins (1988) defined *organizational communication* as the process and structures of communication between persons or positions.

Because organizations are composed of individuals, the need to develop strategic communication to promote organizational change beyond operational change has become apparent (Cutcher, 2009; Gill, 2011). By accepting that employee involvement is central to the organizational change communication process and the subsequent shaping of change outcomes, organizational leaders should become more willing to include a diverse collection of opinions and concerns in the process (Lamm & Gordon, 2010). Communication systems should contain storytelling and narratives to promote dialogue among employees and between employees and organizational leaders (Cutcher, 2009; Driver, 2009).

One school year, I decided to conduct a listening tour with every staff and faculty member on my campus within the first thirty days of school. The rules were simple, and everyone had to participate. At the end of our summer professional training, I drafted an email about my intentions and asked everyone on campus to contact my administrative assistant to schedule a 30-minute meeting with me within the next 30 days. I informed the staff that I would only ask one open-ended question and they would be given free liberty to answer it the way they wanted. I would not be taking notes. I would not sit behind my desk. I would only do one simple thing: I would listen.

Of course, there were some who were thrilled about having my full attention; however, there were some who were disgruntled about being forced to meet with me. All in all, everyone signed up, and I was looking forward to investing in the members on my team. My first appointment began with a hard knock on the door from a staff member who was highly perturbed. They entered my office, rumbling quickly, "I don't need a full 30 minutes, so let's get on with it," as they plopped heavily on my office sofa. I continued smiling and sat on a chair across from them and asked, "What is one thing I need to know that will make your work experience exceptional?" The staff member's head lifted with a face full of surprise. It was as if I had told them they were a millionaire. I showed them my timer and began the time after they began speaking. I was shocked by how much they had to say, and even more shocked when they asked for ten more minutes after the alarm on the timer rang.

I learned a wealth of knowledge about my staff at the conclusion of my listening tour. I learned how many vegan staff members were on campus, how many new parental staff members we had, how many staff members were originally from out of the state, how many staff members spoke more than one language, and the list goes on. I was greatly moved to learn that two of my cafeteria workers began as parent volunteers who decided to join the team well after their children graduated from our school. I learned more from each team member in 30 minutes than I would have ever learned in passing, or during professional development, or in a staff meeting, or at an extracurricular event. It didn't cost me a dime, but my time was well spent. At the end of it all, I learned more about the people. Leading with truth requires you to know the people you are entrusted to lead. The information I gathered helped inform my decisions about policies and practices on campus. For example, a new and simple policy I enacted was the "no email rule" weekdays after 7:00 p.m. or on the weekends. After learning that 80% of my staff members supported their children's athletic and extracurricular activities in the evenings and on the weekends, I decided to discontinue communication during those hours so that people could be free to enjoy spending time with their families. The staff expressed their gratitude. A small change in our communication policy made a big difference. On multiple occasions, staff members shared how happy they were about the little changes we were making. Even better, the year ended with 96% of our staff agreeing to return the following year. This was the highest staff retention rate in the history of the school. Knowing my audience allowed me to become a leader who truthfully adhered to the hearts and minds of my work colleagues. It is a practice that I still employ to this day. Before starting a new project, leading a new course, or facilitating a professional workshop, I lead with truth by understanding my audience, so that I may offer my best leadership services during our collaborative experience.

ACTIVITY #5:
LISTENING TOUR DATA COLLECTION

Journal major findings immediately after each meeting. See the following examples.

Major Findings	Percentage of Staff	Reflection Notes
Staff who are parents	80%	Reduce evening/weekend email communication.
Staff who are non-state natives	20%	Who travels? Who spends holidays alone?
Staff who speak Spanish	60%	Special assets to school community!
Staff who identify as vegan	30%	Important for ordering PD snacks.

FIGURE 4.1 Sample listening tour chart.

Major Findings	Percentage of Staff	Reflection Notes

FIGURE 4.2 Blank listening tour chart.

▶ MAKE THE CONNECTIONS COUNT

Getting to know your staff, students, and parents may potentially lead to everlasting relationships. The truth is that we're all human. Naturally, many of us crave connecting with those who treat us with dignity and respect. Being acknowledged goes far, and it doesn't require much from leaders to do it. One way I tried to learn more about my staff was to simply eat lunch with them and have random conversations. Many school leaders give all their energy towards playground supervision and miss authentic opportunities to make connections with their staff members during their lunch block. I decided to intentionally set time on my calendar to spend at least one day per week enjoying time with the staff in their classrooms, the staff lounge, and sometimes off campus during lunch blocks. I didn't think much of it until I was able to recognize the shift that was occurring between the staff and me. The more we communicated about things that mattered to them outside of school, the more we connected about things that mattered inside the school. My investment in building relationships through genuine discussions was beginning to pay out in various ways staff members supported new initiatives and/ or volunteered to work above and beyond towards common goals. The relationships developed organically and have created some of the most heartfelt memories that will forever be cherished.

During one of my classroom visits, I noticed that one of our fifth-grade teachers was a fan of the same baseball team that my grandad and dad loved, the Los Angeles Dodgers. She was an exemplary teacher who frequently taught lessons that I thoroughly enjoyed observing, but we hadn't organically built the relationship that I was seeking to establish with her as a new administrator to the site. One day during lunch, I peeped in the staff lounge and saw her there sitting alone. I thought it was a good idea to start a conversation about the Dodgers, and boy, did she light up! We talked about how both of our families had established a die-hard generational loyalty to the baseball team. I learned about the moments she spent with her grandmother watching the Dodgers, and I shared how my granddad would sit me on his lap and listen to Vin Scully announce the game on his radio. That magical moment was the beginning of a rewarding, professional connection.

Two years after I transferred to another site, I learned about her grandmother's passing. Immediately, I asked to have dinner with her and her mother. We enjoyed dinner and talked about the many great memories she shared with her grandmother and the Dodgers. She was grateful that I remembered and honored her during a very devastating time in her life. I learned that connections matter. Leading with true conversations requires leaders to make it a point to honor and uplift those whom we have the privilege of leading. To this day, the fifth-grade teacher and I don't get the chance to talk often, but when baseball season is here, we'll be sure to send a text to each other as we cheer on our favorite baseball team. Go, Big Blue!

▶ JOURNAL ACTIVITY: NOTE TO SELF

Instructions: Identify three measurable communication goals that you plan to reach by the end of the next academic semester. Include how you will measure your success and what resources or training you think you will need to be consistent.

REFERENCE LIST

Anjaiah, P., & Sekhar, S. F. (1995). Organizational communication and interpersonal trust: An evaluation of their relationships. *Psychological Studies*, *40*(1), 28–32.

Arsenault, P. (2004). Validating generational differences: A legitimate diversity and leadership issue. *Leadership and Organization Development Journal*, *12*(2), 124–141.

Bourne, B. B. (2009). *Phenomenological study of response to organizational change: Baby boomers, generation X, and generation Y* (Doctoral dissertation). ProQuest Dissertation and Thesis database (UMI No. 3357438).

Brownell, J., & Lundberg, C. C. (1993). The implications of organizational learning for organizational communication: A review and reformulation. *The International Journal of Organizational Analysis*, *1*(1), 29–53.

Burmeister, M. (2008). *From boomers to bloggers: Success strategies across generations*. Synergy Press.

Cutcher, L. (2009). Resisting change from within and without the organization. *Journal of Organizational Change Management, 22,* 275–289. https://doi.org/10/1108/0953481090951069

Driver, M. (2009). From loss to lack: Stories of organizational change as encounters with failed fantasies of self, work and organization. *Organization, 16,* 353–269. https://doi.org/10.1177/1350508409102300

Edstrom, A., & Galbraith, J. (1977). Managerial transfer as a coordination and control strategy. *Administrative Science Quarterly, 22,* 248–263.

Gibson, S. J. (2009). *The zoom guide to generations.* BookSurge.

Gill, R. (2011). Using storytelling to maintain employee loyalty during organizational change. *International Journal of Business and Social Science, 2,* 23–32. http://www.ijbssnet.com/

Goldhaber, G. M. (1974). *Organizational communication.* Wm. C. Brown.

Kappel, A. M. (2012). *Generational cohort as a moderator of the relationship between extrinsic and intrinsic motivation and job satisfaction* (Doctoral dissertation). ProQuest Dissertations and Theses database (UMI No. 3511321).

Krahn, H. J., & Galambos, N. L. (2014). Work values and beliefs of "generation X" and "generation Y". *Journal of Youth Studies, 17,* 92–112.

Lamm, E., & Gordon, J. R. (2010). Empowerment, predisposition to resist change, and support for organizational change. *Journal of Leadership and Organizational Studies, 17,* 426–437.

Lancaster, L. C., & Stillman, D. (2002). *When generations collide: Who they are, why they clash, how to survive the generational puzzle at work.* Harper Business.

Langdon, T. (2012). *Workforce understanding: Multigenerational workforce influence on organizational leadership* (Doctoral dissertation). ProQuest Dissertations and Theses database (UMI No. 3506700).

Lines, R. (2004). Influence of participation in strategic change: Resistance, organizational commitment and change goal achievement. *Journal of Change Management, 4*(3), 193–215.

Loroz, P. S., & Helgeson, J. G. (2013). Boomers and their babies: An exploratory study comparing psychological profiles and advertising appeal effectiveness across two generations. *Journal of Marketing Theory & Practice, 21,* 289–306.

Marcinkus Murphy, W. (2012). Reverse mentoring at work: Fostering cross-generational learning and developing millennial leaders. *Human Resource Management, 51,* 549–573.

McNamara, S. (2005). Incorporating generational diversity. *AORN Journal, 81,* 1149–1153.

Meredith, G., Schewe, C., Hiam, A., & Karlovich, J. (2002). *Managing by defining moments*. Hungry Minds.

Redding, W. C., & Tompkins, P. K. (1988). Organizational communication: Past and present tenses. In G. M. Goldhaber & G. A. Barnett (Eds.), *Handbook of organizational communication* (pp. 5–34). Ablex.

Schultz, R. W. (2010). *Exploring leadership within the modern organization: Understanding the dynamics of effective leadership of virtual, multigenerational workforce* (Doctoral dissertation). ProQuest Dissertations and Theses database (UMI No. 3427471).

Sherman, R. O. (2006). Leading a multigenerational nursing workforce: Issues, challenges, and strategies. *Online Journal of Issues in Nursing, 11*(2), 1.

Yost, S. K. (2013). *Multi-generational perceptions of supervisor leadership, communication, and employee performance* (Doctoral dissertation). ProQuest Dissertations and Theses database (UMI No. 3648732).

5

Understanding Your Conversations

Learning Outcomes for This Chapter

After reading this chapter, you should be able to:

1. Define the four elements of conversational leadership.
2. Assess your conversational competence.
3. Identify evidence of a strong communicator.

Questions to Reflect upon as You Read This Chapter

1. Which element of conversational leadership is your strength?
2. Which element of conversational leadership is your area of potential growth?

Like any researcher, I get all giddy when discussing my area of research expertise. Eleven other doctoral students and I linked up to conduct a thematic research study to examine how exemplary leaders practice conversations through Grosberg and Slind's four elements of conversational leadership: intimacy, interactivity, inclusion, and intentionality (O'Leary, 2018). As defined by educator Carolyn Baldwin states, *conversational leadership* is "the leader's intentional use of conversation as a core process to cultivate the collective intelligence needed to create

> 66 The success of the organization is ultimately achieved by a coalition of folks who align with their beliefs and goals. 99

DOI: 10.4324/9781003325635-7

business and social value." The subpopulation of exemplary leaders that I examined in my research study was nonprofit executive directors. My desire to study this group was led by my understanding of their position in the nonprofit sector as well as the charter school sector. The role of the nonprofit executive director is equivalent to that of the superintendent of schools or the CEO of a business. From past work experience, I also understood that these organizations thrive from being mission-driven. The success of the organization is ultimately achieved by a coalition of folks who align with their beliefs and goals. I was curious to learn more about how these leaders use conversations to motivate, inspire, and support their subordinates. Earlier I mentioned that I minored in communications. In my course of study, I learned the power that effective communication can generate between people. Communication is the gateway to success or conflict in most human interactions. While commonly overlooked, mature leaders are reflective of their conversational competency, but they are also determined to develop strong communication skills across the organizations they lead. To begin, let's review historical leadership styles before diving into the four elements of conversational leadership. From there, we'll explore how other leaders have incorporated conversational leadership practices into their day-to-day interpersonal relationships with stakeholders.

▶ HISTORICAL LEADERSHIP STYLES

The evolution of leadership theories continues to change the way in which leadership competence and self-efficacy are developed and sustained. To understand the significance of the conversational leadership framework, it is important to have a contextual lens of former leadership styles.

Situational Leadership. Situational leadership theory (SLT) is a highly recognized theory in the field of managerial leadership (Meier, 2016). Chaneski (2016) described SLT as four leadership styles that are applicable based on specific situations: directing, coaching, supporting, and delegating. Chaneski claimed that adopting the right leadership style to manage situational occurrences with employees will inevitably create easier opportunities for leaders to guide their employees to the desired outcomes.

Authentic Leadership. *Authentic leadership* is defined as a pattern of leader behavior that draws upon and promotes both positive psychological capacities and a positive ethical climate to foster greater self-awareness, an internalized moral perspective, balanced processing of information, and relational transparency on the part of leaders working with followers, fostering positive self-development (Walumbwa et al., 2008, p. 94).

Transformational Leadership. Transformation leadership theory has been one of the most recognized topics in the field of leadership research (Raj & Srivastava, 2016). Transformational leaders motivate their followers and bring awareness about the importance and value of designated outcomes and the ways of achieving those outcomes (Bass & Avolio, 2004). Transformational leadership requires exceptional influence that motivates followers to perform above and beyond the required expectations (Marques, 2007). Raj and Srivastava (2016) asserted that transformational leaders empower and encourage employees to try new things, for example, new ways of communicating.

▶ FOUR ELEMENTS OF CONVERSATIONAL LEADERSHIP

The idea of conversational leadership is a relatively new leadership approach (Nichols, 2012). From this explanation, J. Brown and Hurley (2009) developed a framework for exercising conversational leadership. According to this framework, leaders establish effective conversation by implementing six architectures for engagement. From this perspective, conversations are multidimensional (Glaser, 2014) and require a deeper understanding of how people develop and sustain healthy conversations. Additionally, Glaser (2014) discovered that conversational gaps, communication through emotional fear, occur when a lack of connectivity is exchanged between those in conversation. Through intentional and intimate conversations, these gaps can be reduced once trust is established (Glaser, 2014).

Adding to the conversational leadership narrative is Groysberg and Slind's (2012a) research in organizational dynamics. In their attempt to investigate how people communicate in twenty-first-century organizations, they discovered that creating organizational conversation was no longer an option for executive leaders (Groysberg & Slind, 2012a). From this view, Groysberg and Slind defined *smart leaders* as those who "understand that they can't avoid conversation nor can they control it, but if they engage with it in the right way, they have the potential to unleash organizational energy that no leader could ever demand" (p. 9). After two years of extensive research with executive leaders in a variety of organizations, Groysberg and Slind (2012b) developed a model that uses communicative indicators to shift the focus of corporate communication from a top-down distribution to a bottom-up exchange of ideas. According to Groysberg and Slind (2012a, 2012b), the four essential elements in developing organizational conversation are intimacy, interactivity, inclusion, and intentionality. Organizational leaders who establish these conversation-based practices tend to receive high levels of employee engagement and outperform their industry counterparts (Groysberg & Slind, 2012a).

Intimacy. Intimate conversations involve an exchange in dialogue between participants where there is implementation of active listening skills. Groysberg and Slind (2012a) believed that the most powerful trait gained from intimate conversations is trust.

Interactivity. Interactivity is "a continuous construct capturing the quality of two-way communication between two parties" (Alba et al., 1997, p. 38). Interactivity allows the process of dialogue to occur between leaders and employees without the fear of negative consequences.

Inclusion. In this role, employees are encouraged to share their ideas and contribute to rich conversations related to critical decisions within the organization. Inclusion creates a shared responsibility for all members. Passionate employees become living representatives of the company and serve as brand ambassadors (Groysberg & Slind, 2012a).

Intentionality. Different from the other three components, intentionality requires transparency and honesty from leaders. In this area, leaders openly share their intentions for the organization and their vision for success. Groysberg and Slind (2012a) believed that employee buy-in may increase when they have opportunities to participate in strategic planning and development. Creating multilevel participation in the early conversations of strategic planning promotes a shared vision across the organization.

Using the common theme of conversational leadership, our group of researchers interviewed 9–12 participants from each of our subpopulations. We developed interview questions that we would all use to collect our qualitative data. The interview process was captivating. Through my own professional networks and word of mouth, I was able to meet with ten extraordinary nonprofit executive directors throughout Los Angeles County. Some gave me tours of their organization, others provided me with artifacts, and a few allowed me to participate in some of the activities their organizations hosted at the time of my visit. One key pattern that I immediately observed from all the participants was their passion for the work they were leading. From food banks to parent advocacy to college preparation programs for underprivileged students and everything in between, these leaders were fired up for their cause. Their zeal was truly electric.

Another pattern that I quickly observed was the way in which they communicated with their staff or their clients. It was clear that the rapport they displayed was genuine and real. The people we encountered formally or informally truly liked connecting with their leaders. By the time I sat down to talk with each of them, I was very excited to learn more about their perceived communication styles with their followers.

Zumdahl (2010) highlighted the reinforcing idea that:

> [L]eaders must both have a combination of a skill set that can be adapted to a variety of situations and some inherent characteristics and knowledge that gives them the ability and drive to be effective in their positions at the top of organizations.
>
> (p. 38)

The mark of an effective leader is his or her ability to discern and adapt to varying levels of need (Uzonwanne, 2007). Edwards and Yankey (2006) claimed that leaders must deal with complexities in society that require a diverse set of management skills.

During our time together, many participants shared some touching reflections about different times when they implemented intimacy, interactivity, inclusion, or intentionality. These stories were deep and real testaments to the power of leading with truth. I invite you to read four short testimonials from my research interviews. Immediately when you're done reading, please take a moment to reflect on when you've exhibited the four elements of conversational leadership. Which element do you exhibit well? Which element do you need more growth on? After your reflections, create and share the survey questions in Activity #6 to learn how your staff members perceive your conversational leadership practices.

Conversational Leadership Case Study #1

Intimacy is defined as the closeness, trust, and familiarity created between people through shared experiences, meaningful exchanges, and shared knowledge.

I think for me being able to share an honest story about growing up, and even though I'm in a position of leadership for an organization that focuses on writing and literacy and education, I didn't start off in a place where that was where I thought I'd end up. For me, the drive has been really to improve myself and to maybe inspire young people to see that. They have time to figure themselves out, and we should never label kids in any way. Sharing those kinds of intimate details about my own upbringing and growth is really where I've been focused. It not only helps me connect with my staff but, I think, also really helps them know that I'm here. In fact, when you are working in a nonprofit, you are not here for the paycheck; you are here to help with the mission. I do think that when you are honest about your own circumstances and where you come from, it really connects inversely to your team and to others.

Research Conclusion for Intimacy

Leaders who want to provide an intimate, trusting work environment must lead by example and share personal stories to establish relevancy.

Conversational Leadership Case Study #2

Inclusion is defined as the commitment to the process of engaging stakeholders to share ideas and participate in the development of the organization.

We recently had an event here, and oftentimes, in those kinds of events, the executive director would welcome people or at least be onstage at a certain point during the presentation. But in fact, I sat in the back and let the whole thing be run by people who actually put it all together. Not many of them had ever had that opportunity before, and they were looking nervous. Show that you have faith in them and that you allow room for mistakes because we all learn by making mistakes. When people make mistakes, the response is not yelling and screaming. Help them learn something. Help them make sure they don't do it the next time.

Research Conclusion for Inclusion

Leaders who value inclusion should seek active contributions from all stakeholders.

Conversational Leadership Case Study #3

Interactivity is defined as the bilateral or multilateral exchange of comments and ideas, a back-and-forth process.

By establishing that safe space, we were all able to come as ourselves and be honest. We had some pretty intimate conversations, and I was able to really also listen very closely and feel and understand how others in my team had encountered moments of racism or feeling excluded, not feeling like another. I think it really helped me and the rest of the team feel closer and to also get a better sort of understanding not only about what we are dealing with but also about what our students bring in.

Research Conclusion for Interactivity

Leaders who create safe spaces for their employees to communicate openly to express their views will develop organizations where information sharing is embedded within the culture.

Conversational Leadership Case Study #4

Intentionality is defined as ensuring clarity of purpose that includes goals and direction to create order and meaning.

We went through a strategic planning process a few years ago, and I was told by consultants that this is your vision, this is an opportunity for you to really push your idea of what you want for the organization moving forward. It didn't sit well with me. I don't know if that's typical of all foci of consultancy on how a strategic plan should evolve. Obviously, I know that a big chunk of what's happening is my vision, but I've always been somebody who wanted to create a sense of giving people an opportunity to really voice their ideas. I decided to go a different route, and I certainly wanted to bring in the opinions of not only my staff but also student voices, family voices, volunteer voices, and of course, the board as well.

Research Conclusion for Intentionality

Leaders who intentionally seek to demonstrate the mission of their organization must monitor awareness of common purpose by soliciting feedback from all stakeholders.

▶ FEEDBACK LEADS TO TRUE CHANGE

After an evaluation on my job, I took time to review and reflect upon the information other employers stated about my performance. All school administrators were asked to include their immediate supervisor, direct reports, and colleagues in an email survey. To receive a true and honest analysis on my performance as a school leader, I made sure to include multiple stakeholders that would represent a broad range of perspectives within our school community. I was genuinely interested in how people viewed my leadership abilities, so that I may improve and grow in areas of need. The evaluation process first required me to complete the survey as a self-analysis of my performance. The survey was very simplistic. It consisted of 30 questions with available responses ranging from "never" to "always." The end of the survey allowed opportunity for the evaluator to add additional information as desired. All in all, it took approximately 15 to 20 minutes for me to complete. Now that step 1 was complete, it was time for me to wait to receive the survey evaluations from the staff.

Nervous, excited, and anxious all at the same time, I was eager to review the results. Just as I was about to click open the email with all 17 responses, the voice of doubt began softly whispering in my ear, saying, "What if they don't like you?" "How would you continue working with your staff?" "What if they responded negatively?" "Was this a good idea?" After all, why was I so enthusiastic about what people had to say about me? I was confident, sharp, and competent in my skill sets. I did not require anyone to validate my worth as an employee . . . or did I? It was in this moment I was reminded of one of the attributes which distinguished and set me apart from my peers, and that was my flexibility to adapt to change. My desire to review the survey responses was not for purposes of flattery, self-righteousness, or self-pity but rather to understand my areas of strengths and weaknesses from the perspective of those surrounding me. I desired to grow. I wanted to improve my ability to demonstrate strong leadership even if it meant changing and adapting to the school culture as a vested partner. In her book *Mindset*, world-renowned Stanford University psychologist Carol Dweck identifies flexible people as those who possess a growth mindset.

If you believe you can develop yourself, then you're open to accurate information about your current abilities, even if it's unflattering. What's more, if you're oriented towards learning, then you need accurate information about your current abilities to learn effectively. If we lead with truth, then we set the standards that we expect all partners to follow in developing a healthy learning environment. If we desire to teach children how to be resilient in challenging situations and how to possess the ability to adapt to unforeseen and seen situations, then it must start with the adults on campus. We, the educator, must possess the ability to think swiftly about the day-to-day obstacles in our schools. To be effective with this pursuit, we must be willing to develop ourselves by accurately reflecting on our strengths and weaknesses and be willing to adapt to the needs of our school community. This is an essential breaking point to a healthy school transformation.

ACTIVITY #6:
CONVERSATIONAL LEADERSHIP SURVEY

Create a Google survey using the following questions and distribute to members you lead.

Use the data to pivot or enhance your conversational leadership practices

1. Using the following scale, rate how often your leader promotes trust between them and the members of the organization.
   Never Occasionally Always
2. Using the following scale, rate how often your leader listens actively to the members of the organization to engage in honest and authentic conversations.
   Never Occasionally Always
3. Using the following scale, rate how often your leader engages in conversations with members in the organization that are two-way exchanges of ideas and information about your organization.
   Never Occasionally Always
4. Using the following scale, rate how often your leader effectively promotes conversations with members of your organization that incorporated an exchange of ideas about a difficult topic or issue.
   Never Occasionally Always
5. Using the following scale, rate how often your leader uses effective strategies to ensure members of the organization remain committed to the organization's mission.
   Never Occasionally Always
6. Using the following scale, rate how often your leader encourages all members to become active contributors and spokespersons for the organization.
   Never Occasionally Always
7. Using the following scale, rate how often your leader uses conversation to create clarity around your organization's purpose.
   Never Occasionally Always
8. Using the following scale, rate how often your leader uses conversation to elicit feedback on the goals and direction of your organization.
   Never Occasionally Always

▶ TRUTH CREATES CHANGE EVOLUTION

An expected outcome of leading with truth is change. As leaders begin to get back to their why, understand their hearts, prioritize their core values, learn their audiences, and communicate effectively with their teams, they inevitably begin to evolve. This change evolution will begin to shift the environment and contagiously evoke others to walk, live, and breathe out truth. Can you imagine a world where people displayed truth? Even if their beliefs, manners, and values differed from yours, wouldn't it be refreshing to engage with colleagues in the most authentic version of themselves? Truth is compatible with identity. The more we accept the truth about others, the safer they would feel in revealing who they are and what matters most to them. Leaders who use conversations to create a workflow where truth is welcomed are usually recipients of having team members who are genuinely anchored in supporting the goals of the school. Teachers, parents, and students have repeatedly shared testimonials about the impact of inclusive school spaces that truly cared about their humanity. In these moments, we have learned that leaders who make the most impact in the lives of those they serve are competent in leading through conversations that yield true feedback, true connections with all, and true results. Let's continue to evolve by allowing truth to change us.

▶ JOURNAL ACTIVITY: NOTE TO SELF

Instructions: Analyze the data from the conversational leadership survey to create three measurable communication goals. Identify how you will determine when you have successfully achieved each goal.

REFERENCE LIST

Alba, J., Lynch, J., Weitz, B., Janiszewski, C., Lutz, R., Sawyer, A., & Wood, S. (1997). Interactive home shopping: Consumer, retailer, and manufacturer incentives to participate in electronic marketplaces. *Journal of Marketing, 61*, 38–53.

Bass, B. M., & Avolio, B. J. (2004). *Manual for the multifactor leadership questionnaire*. Mind Garden.

Brown, J., & Hurley, T. (2009). Conversation leadership: Thinking together for a change. *Pegasus Communications, 20*(9), 2–7.

Chaneski, W. (2016, October 12). Employing the right leadership style. *Modern Machine Shop*. www.mmsonline.com/columns/employing-the-rightleadership-style

Edwards, R. L., & Yankey, J. A. (2006). *Effectively managing nonprofit organizations*. NASW Press.

Glaser, J. E. (2014). *Conversational intelligence*. Bibliomotion.

Groysberg, B., & Slind, M. (2012a). Leadership is a conversation: Talking with employees, rather than to them, can promote operational flexibility, employee engagement, and tight strategic alignment. *Harvard Business Journal, 90*(6), 76–85.

Groysberg, B., & Slind, M. (2012b). *Talk, Inc.: How trusted leaders use conversation to power their organizations*. Harvard Business Review Press.

Marques, J. F. (2007). On impassioned leadership: A comparison between leaders from divergent walks of life. *International Journal of Leadership Studies, 3*(1), 98–125.

Meier, D. (2016). Situational leadership theory as a foundation for a blended learning framework. *Journal of Education and Practice, 7*(10), 25–30.

Nichols, S. (2012). *Cultivating intentional conversations: A narrative study of those who lead through the use of conversation in their spheres of influence* (Doctoral dissertation). ProQuest Dissertations and Theses database (UMI No. 3546096).

O'Leary, Q. (2018). *Conversational leadership: A leadership approach for nonprofit executive directors* (Dissertations 187). https://digitalcommons.umassglobal.edu/edd_dissertations/187

Raj, R., & Srivastava, K. B. L. (2016). Transformational leadership and innovativeness: The mediating role of organizational learning. *Journal of Management Research, 16*(4), 201–219.

Uzonwanne, F. (2007). *Leadership style and decision-making models among corporate leaders in non-profit organizations* (Doctoral dissertation). ProQuest Dissertations and Theses database (UMI No. 3278086).

Walumbwa, F. O., Avolio, B. J., Gardner, W. L., Wernsing, T. S., & Peterson, S. J. (2008). Authentic leadership: Development and validation of a theory-based measure. *Journal of Management, 34*(1), 89–126.

Zumdahl, L. E. (2010). *The perceived managerial and leadership effectiveness of nonprofit leaders* (Doctoral dissertation). ProQuest Dissertations and Theses database (UMI No. 3410325).

Part 3
Lead with True Experiences

6

Understanding
Your Work
Culture

Learning Outcomes for This Chapter

After reading this chapter, you should be able to:

1. Recognize the impact of work culture.
2. Identify the value of student voice on your campus.
3. Identify the value of parent/family voice on your campus.

Questions to Reflect upon as You Read This Chapter

1. How do you assess school climate? Is the data accurate and true?
2. How do teachers connect with each other beyond required meetings?

Like the temperature in your home, one can feel the climate of your work environment immediately upon entrance. When the temperature we feel differs from what we expect, we naturally begin to find ways to make adjustments that fit our levels of comfort. This is called trusting our gut instinct or intuition. One of my mentors advised me early in my leadership career that "everything communicates something." I didn't really understand it at that time, but as I reflected more on effective culture-building practices, I began to observe significant

DOI: 10.4324/9781003325635-9

connections between school climate and student achievement. The revelation was mind-blowing and catapulted my ability to lead transformational initiatives. Before reaching my peak of success, I first had to ask and acknowledge the truth about my work culture and ask questions such as: Did I have a false idea of my school's climate? Did the children like learning on their campus? Did the teachers and faculty feel appreciated? Did the families and community members feel welcomed and included? The answers to many of these questions could not be arrived at by a single end-of-year school climate survey. As a matter of fact, these questions required intentional efforts that needed time, attentive listening, funding, reflection, and action. Tackling the road not taken meant one word: SACRIFICE. Now, I ask you, What are you willing to sacrifice to ensure the children, faculty, and families experience a positive and healthy school culture? For me, it was important that we all adopted a "go hard or go home" mentality towards building our educational paradise.

Educational paradise is a phrase I coined to describe the characteristics of a wonderful place to teach and learn. Think about what comes to mind when you hear the word *paradise*. For me, I think of warm, sunny weather. I think about deep blue oceans. I hear laughter from children splashing in the water. I see photos being snapped and games being played. I feel relaxed and peaceful. It brings me pure joy when I think about paradise. Consider your last vacation or a vacation you have on your bucket list. I recall my last vacation in San Juan, Puerto Rico. I took my daughter, Kyla, and her bestie with me to celebrate my 40th birthday. My business partner later joined us to help celebrate the milestone occasion. The only request I asked our group was to be on the beach and to eat some good seafood on my actual birthday. The day was perfect for me, but the image I recall that gives me the greatest pleasure to this day was the sight of my daughter's best friend, Chele, floating in the deep ocean without a care in the world. At some point, our group and neighboring beachgoers stopped what they were doing to observe how carefree Chele appeared while enjoying the atmosphere. She floated far out, so it was a sight to witness. I knew that she was an excellent swimmer, so I wasn't worried. We just let her float. That young college student was truly experiencing paradise. From that point, I started thinking about what a school campus would look like if all students were, like Chele, floating from class to class, happily enjoying their learning environment. What conversations would be expressed in the staff lounge between teachers who were passionately teaching content in meaningful ways? How could parents find joy in supporting events and sharing their talents in the school community? If you want to lead your school to becoming an educational paradise, you must assess where your school culture is currently to develop a road map to your final school culture destination.

▶ DATA RIDES SHOTGUN

As a little girl, I always wanted to ride in the shotgun seat whenever my dad was driving. The shotgun passenger rode in the front seat and helped him smoothly drive us from one destination to the next. Before there was Siri, the shotgun passenger helped with reading the map, twisted the cap off Dad's soda bottle since his hands were glued to the wheel, changed the dial on radio until we heard his jam, and kept him alert with random conversations about everything we saw on the road. In those moments it was just me and my dad. Nothing or no one else mattered. We were best friends who relied on each other to get us to the end of our journey safely, soundly, and on time. One of my first discoveries in leadership occurred after I gave my school data the shotgun seat. I learned how to use disaggregated data to give me clues to challenges preventing our children from growing academically. These clues led to questions and concerns about certain learners who repeatedly demonstrated disproportionate outcomes from their counterparts. Data-driven decision-making is the process by which an individual collects, examines, and interprets empirical evidence for the purpose of deciding (Mandinach & Jackson, 2012). I knew I needed more data to help me navigate receiving accurate answers to my questions, but it was going to take time and strategy. Knowing this, our leadership team decided to take a different approach rather than solely rely on quantitative state assessments and grade book scores. Blankstein and Houston (2010) assert that enhanced decisions lead to an enhanced quality of student life. We knew that we needed to hear from the people. We knew that we needed to capture the truth about how people felt about our school community. We knew that we needed them to believe their voices mattered, and as leaders, we knew we would lead with truth to create a workplace that mirrored our shared values and educational beliefs. Once we identified our goals for attaining an inclusive and equitable environment, we began to strategically design a game plan of action.

▶ HITTING A GRAND SLAM

In the game of baseball, a *grand slam* refers to a team scoring as many runs as possible in one at bat. Hitting a grand slam is rare and renders immediate praise from all who witness the moment. To set up a grand slam moment, the general manager must carefully consider a batting lineup that could potentially lead to bases loaded. *Bases loaded*, simply put, means there is a runner on the first base, a runner on the second base, and a runner on the third base. This setup puts the batter at the plate in position to hit a grand slam that would automatically advance all runners to the home plate to score.

One of the greatest moments in the history of the Boston Red Sox franchise occurred during the 1999 ALDS game 5 against the Cleveland Indians. The Red Sox were down, and their franchise pitcher was sitting out with a back injury. The chances of winning were looking very slim for the Red Sox team. It wasn't until the third inning when light began to shed on the Boston players. One by one, players made advancements to first base, eventually leading up to bases loaded. Through strategic planning and grit, the Boston Red Sox set themselves up for a grand slam moment. Troy O'Leary was up next to grace the plate. On the first pitch, Troy swung the bat and drove the ball into deep-right field for a grand slam, putting his team up 4–1. The Red Sox won the game and advanced to the ACLS after starting the series in a 2–0 deficit. It was a game to remember and will forever be hailed by all baseball fanatics from generation to generation.

I remember watching that game in my college dormitory in complete astonishment. To this day, it continues to impact my life in a major way. As a teacher, school administrator, mother, and community advocate, I have always aimed to create grand slam moments in my life. Like a baseball general manager,

I have learned how to lead with truth to skillfully and strategically set up golden opportunities to advance myself from my current position. I call this process grand slam strategies, which will be later discussed . For now, I'm going to focus on the big moment when our leadership team hit the ball out of the park!

Now, before jumping in headfirst to discuss the big moment, let's discuss the three bases for culture change that our leadership team completed.

Base 1. Our leadership team had to *acknowledge* that the temperature in our school's environment needed adjustment. In far too many cases, I've observed everyone on campus experiencing school culture toxicity except the leaders. Whether it's denial, fatigue, or lack of ability, leaders must be honest with themselves by recognizing the discomfort others are experiencing. While this truth may sting at first, it will help lead to the second step, which is to collect and review data about your organization's stakeholders.

Leaders must decide to be active listeners and believe that everyone has the right to be heard. Equity-conscious leaders place a high value on all members while creating an atmosphere of common goals. This requires practice, patience, and persistence, but the outcomes are worth the investment.

> **"**Real climate change in schools begin with *collecting data* about the people you serve and the people in the organization who serve alongside you.**"**

Base 2. Real climate change in schools begin with *collecting data* about the people you serve and the people in the organization who serve alongside you. This could be collected through quantitative survey data, but I strongly encourage leaders to conduct small-group and individual interviews. Qualitative interviews capture the depths of how people feel about their environment. I've discovered that these authentic and intimate conversations have provided me with more insight beyond stats on paper. Nonverbal communication has equally been a beneficial tool to assist with understanding the thoughts and feelings of my colleagues. Over the years, I've learned that when people believe that you care, they will care to speak to you about the matters of their heart.

For example, I recall one year informing my staff that one of my goals for the year was to improve my active listening skills. This meant that I wanted their honest opinion of my listening skills immediately after a large-group conversation and after small, intimate conversations. I explained to the team that I was asking for an exchange of trust. I needed an opportunity to be vulnerable enough to receive feedback, and I needed them to be courageous enough to tell me the truth without fear of retaliation. This was a big leap of shifting our culture from a top-down environment to shared community, where every person had a safe space to strengthen their professional skills. This trust exchange was a fundamental value in shifting our school climate. Once the trust exchange is established, it's time to move to the third step, which is to transfer data into action.

Base 3. *Strategic planning* can be summed up in one word: intentionality. Intentionality is being deliberate and purposeful in everything you do. Intentionality requires transparency and honesty from leaders. In this area, leaders openly share their intentions for the organization and their vision for success. Wise leaders employ strategy as a tool that guides them towards achieving their desired outcomes. To generate a positive workspace, strategic design should include deliberate practices that include substantial feedback from all stakeholders. Skipping this step could potentially lead to Peter Drucker's popular quote: "Culture eats strategy for breakfast."

A particular instance when this occurred was when my former principal and I transitioned from the school where we served together. We both had been promoted to new roles at new sites. In partnership, we spent three years developing systems and structures that not only supported the mission of the school but, equally important, also supported the campus culture. Through establishing trusting relationships with seasoned staff members and families who had been a part of the school's inception, we were able to understand the history and values of the school community. Jokingly, I refer to these as "golden calves," which refers to the traditions and ceremonial customs of a school culture that should be carefully considered before eliminating. For example, this school held an annual father-daughter dance. The dance had been hosted by the school's PTA as one of their signature fundraising events. In other words, it was a big deal for the teachers, the students, and the parents. Altering this event with this school community could have sparked a significant backlash requiring unnecessary damage control. It was this advice that my principal and I passed on to the new administrative team that was preparing to acquire the leadership roles at our school. One of the pieces of advice I specifically shared was to maintain implementation of the current master schedule. The school's unique magnet program presented previous challenges that our faculty and district personnel had finally been able to overcome and reach amicable agreement on. I presented the current master schedule to the new administrators and offered additional training to help with understanding the nuances of the master schedule. After agreeing to continue implementation of the existing master schedule for at least one year, the new principal had a change of heart. Instead of following our advice, the principal decided to go in a different direction and, rightfully, had every right to do so. In their opinion, they wanted to take the school in a different direction and decided to make immediate changes. While I wholeheartedly believe their intentions were pure, their decisions ultimately led to many challenges between them and the faculty. In this case, the structural changes were eaten for breakfast by the climate of the school culture and its members.

The presence of buy-in within the members of the organization develops genuine interest to support the change initiatives required to change the school environment temperature. Leading with truth is worth emulating. When leaders avoid honest reflection and assessment of the environment they serve, it negatively impacts their team. Unfortunately, this may deplete the zeal that has inspired them to lead. It creates mundane leaders. A mundane leader is someone who goes through the motion of leading without possessing positive connections with the members they're leading. Leaders have a responsibility to create working conditions that allows everyone to thrive. What does that look like in action? What conditions have you recently created that equitably allows all members on your campus to thrive?

▶ BASES LOADED: SETTING UP THE GRAND SLAM MOMENT

Let's recap. To set up a grand slam moment, we need to make sure we have all bases covered. We mentioned that reaching the first base requires campus leaders to first acknowledge the toxicities that exist on their campus. One way to understand this in a clear, objective manner is to round towards second base by collecting data. Data collection should be triangular, encompassing interviews, observations, and artifacts, to help leaders develop a well-informed data analysis. Heading towards third base requires leaders to use data analysis to drive strategic development. The process of developing strategies is most effective when buy-in from all stakeholders occurs. Once all three bases are loaded, the school is in position for their grand slam moment. Grand slam moments will vary from school to school. For one school, the grand slam moment could mean an increase in student enrollment as a direct result of an improved student culture. For another school, a grand slam moment could be an increase in teacher retention as a direct result of teachers feeling like their voices matter. In every case, a school's grand slam moment should lead to growth in student achievement. This is the primary goal. Systems and structures should promote safe and caring learning spaces that produce growth in student achievement and acceleration.

In the end, the environment you will create will determine your leadership legacy. What leadership legacy are you creating? How will people remember your impact on the organization? Leaders who lead with truth are historically admired, respected, and never forgotten. In the face of controversy, here's my leadership quote playlist of what great leaders say about leading with truth:

> *If you don't like something, change it. If you can't change it, change your attitude.*
>
> —Maya Angelou

> *You will make all kinds of mistakes; but as long as you are generous and true and also fierce you cannot hurt the world or even seriously distress her.*
>
> —Winston Churchill

> *Life's most persistent and urgent question is, "What are you doing for others?"*
>
> —Dr. Martin Luther King Jr

It is the responsibility of intellectuals to speak the truth and expose lies.

—Noam Chomsky

Integrity is telling myself the truth. And honesty is telling the truth to other people.

—Spencer Johnson

Great communication begins with connection.

—Oprah Winfrey

Change will not come if we wait for some other person or some other time. We are the ones we've been waiting for. We are the change that we seek.

—Barack Obama

The decision to lead in truth will yield your most remarkable results by igniting others to produce their most creative workmanship. Truth earns trust, and trust reduces emotional filters while increasing innovative genius. #LeadershipFacts.

ACTIVITY #7:
LEADERSHIP QUOTE PLAYLIST

Identify five to seven quotes about leadership and truth. Print them out and let them serve as a daily reminder.

Playlist Example

Quote	Author
Great communication begins with connection.	**Oprah Winfrey**
It is the responsibility of intellectuals to speak the truth and expose lies.	**Noam Chomsky**

▶ LADIES LEADING LEGACIES: A PRINCIPAL'S CONVERSATION

In the fall of 2021, I invited a few colleagues to join a webinar discussion hosted by my educational firm, Minty Educational

Services. The purpose of the panel was to share the educational leadership perspective through the lens of female principals of color. The goal was to reflect on their lived experience as school leaders in the global pandemic to gain insight on how they have sustained healthy campus cultures while addressing the crisis of academic gaps and teacher shortage concerns. As you read our intimate, transcribed conversation, learn about their "lead with truth leadership" moments to discover ideas, tips, or best practices you may consider adopting on your campus to strengthen or sustain a positive school culture.

Background of Participants

Principal 1. A turnaround Texas principal. Previously, she spent time as a speech and language instructor and has also spent time as a school counselor. Additionally, she is part-time entrepreneur with business consulting and a real estate. Her leadership quote is, "Prepare yourself and expect greatness. I've seen too many victories to believe defeat will have the last word."

Principal 2. Bridges her love for teaching community and scholar activism. Representing California, she has over four years of classroom instruction and has spent seven years as a high school administrator and director of curriculum and instruction. She is also committed to teaching postsecondary courses centered on ethnic studies critical pedagogy, healing justice, and diversity, equity, and inclusion (DEI).

Principal 3. Representing Texas, she has 10 years of classroom instruction and 21 years as a school principal. She has recently celebrated 31 years in education and has been an elementary school leader for grades pre-K through fifth. Her leadership quote is, "Leaders have an opportunity to make an impact on our children and school communities like never before."

Principal 4. Representing California, she has spent 20 years of classroom instruction and serves as an induction mentor for aspiring teachers. She has four years of school administrator experience and is actively pursuing her doctoral degree.

Principal 5. Representing California, she has 15 years of classroom instruction and seven years serving as a school administrator. She is currently the leader in district-wide equity initiatives, and her leadership quote is, "All involved stakeholders should continue building relationships as foundations for student success to help prepare our students to become global citizens who are career- and college-ready."

Principal 6. Representing Maryland, she has eight years of classroom instruction, nine years as an assistant principal, and 22 years as principal. She is currently celebrating her 40th year in education and has two amazing daughters currently serving in education; one daughter is a school administrator, and her other daughter is a classroom teacher.

The Discussion

Question 1. Let's talk about the 2020 global pandemic. What has been the most challenging, and are things getting better?

Principal 1. *The overall impact on students being socially, emotionally, and academically disconnected for nearly 18 months, and now having to work to reacclimate them to structured learning environments, daily routines, academic expectations— I personally feel like that's been a huge challenge for us all. Additionally, you know educators are always addressing learning gaps, but now even more than ever, we have a huge undertaking in working with learning gaps of our students and the amount of instructional time that we lost during the pandemic. It is really requiring us to, you know, constantly pivot and embrace the changes, remain flexible, and do some things that we've never really done just to meet the individual needs of our students. So personally, from my vantage point, that's been my experience, but as educators, we're always up for the challenge, because that's what we do.*

Principal 4. *I would just like to add that it's also been hard on our teachers having to come back. There's been a lot of expectations placed on them, and so something that we've tried to do for our teachers is like a "no work" weekend. No sending emails and no communicating with them, to make sure that they're taking care of their health. Also, they're the ones that have to come on Monday to teach our students, so we're really making sure that our teachers are healthy. Our district has provided a lot of time for them to exercise and having them think about their social-emotional state so they can support our students. Also, within the social-emotional [context], if our teachers are not doing well, then our students are not going to do well.*

Principal 3. At the very beginning, just the doing virtual was very interesting. Even though we had one-to-one with iPads and laptops in all the children's hands, it was still a challenge with internet services in some areas and so forth. Then we got through that. Now we're back; 'bout 95% our students are back face-to-face. Some of them have requested to be at home because of medical reasons and so forth, but for the most part, we're all back. Do we have learning gaps? Most definitely. There are learning gaps. I will say something very positive I heard this last week from one of my younger teachers. Early on, when we started the school year, I said we've got to remember that as we begin the year, let's be as positive as we can and let's not constantly talk about those gaps, because then we're just kind of reinforcing that. You know, have the mentality of the glass half-full instead of half-empty. I encouraged the staff to let's go into the school year like this. The teacher told me on Tuesday, when I met with him, "I know we do have learning gaps, but I'll tell you something, the kids are willing to learn." So even though the gaps are there, it's as if this year and a half has also created in the children that willingness and that eagerness to come back. That eagerness to have normalcy in their lives, appreciation for school, and appreciation for teachers. Discipline is way down, and are we working hard. Most definitely pivot. One of the other ladies said that word, pivot. Oh my gosh! Isn't that the name of the game this year? Pivot! Pivot! Pivot! You got to keep a smile on your face while you're doing it. So it's been an interesting one for me. It's been challenging, but I'll tell you, I don't do anything like I used to do. I had been doing this for 21 years. I had created files where I had my beginning-of-the-year, middle-of-the-year, end-of-the-year events that I always did. [In the past] I just went to my little pretty little file, prettied it up a little bit, changed the date, and there, we're ready to go. I don't think I've opened three-fourths of those files. I've done everything different. We're gonna have a trick-or-treat. Like a trunk-or-treat on our campus. It's going to be a literacy night tomorrow. It's nothing we've ever done before. Everything's new, so it has added that, and we're just trying to get back to normal as much as we can for our children, for our community, and for our teachers. It's all about the people.

Question 2. How do we heal our schools after a pandemic? Specifically, address student healing, staff healing, and self-healing.

Principal 5. *Student healing, of course, starts with not only building relationships but [also] rebuilding those relationships. As mentioned earlier, students have been out of school for 15 months, so we must continue to have those constant building of relationships with students. We have to capture their hearts. Capturing Kids Hearts is a program we have at our school site where we're building those relationships and providing positive and behavior supports. We need more SELS on campus, social and emotional learning specialists, which, since the pandemic and coming back to campus, our school district has provided an SEL on every single campus for us, because there is a dire need for having that successful SEL program. So when it comes to student healing, social-emotional learning specialist is the key to help those students develop socially. Relearn how to socialize because they are having to relearn how to socialize. Providing them with those supports so that they can learn in the classroom.*

Principal 3. *You know what? I completely agree with what you said. Relationships [are] at the foundation. We must build relationships with our children. Making sure that they're safe, that they feel safe, because some of them were nervous about coming back. Some of them still get worried when someone brushes up against their backpack. They feel like they've got to spray it down, so there are things obviously that we've got to deal with not only now but in the future [as well]. We also have a social-emotional counselor on our campus. It's only a half-time position, but you know what? That half-time counselor has made such a huge difference because our counselor was swamped as it is, and then with the needs of this whole pandemic, we were able to get this additional [half-time] counselor, which allows us to provide counseling all week. They see the classes 45 minutes each, which means every class gets group counseling. It's a guidance lesson, and they do dancing, and they just make it fun and just talk, and it's a really good time for them. They get to do that twice a week. So they get a counselor for twice a week, and of course, we've got the small group. Then we also have the one-to-one. That is really [a] need. That is just the bottom of it. Just trying to bring in little activities of little time at the park. Things that we can still do safely and just put a smile on kids' faces and have that balance for them.*

Principal 5. *When it comes to staff healing, that is essential. If your staff is not healed, your students aren't going to get the healing, as mentioned earlier. So you know, keeping teachers in the loop is very important. Transparency is key. You don't want your teachers caught off guard with a new protocol, or a new policy, or a new change in the district. So you want to always make sure that you're a transparent leader in providing a plethora of team-building activities to constantly build staff relationships. Also, provide teachers with all the resources and supports that they need, because really, as the leader and the principal of the school, you're working for them. You're there for them. You're providing everything that they need, like materials, supports, and resources, so that they can do what they need to do so that our children are successful. When we lead, we lead from the middle. Really, we're not at the top, and we're not at the bottom. We lead from the middle because it's really our teachers who make children successful, so having those supports and resources that they need and sharing ideas of self-healing techniques in staff meetings is also very helpful.*

Principal 3. *It's all about servant leadership. It really is. Right now, more than ever. For the last 20 years, leadership was about "Be in the classrooms" and "You have to be in the hallways," but this is at another level. It's more of a calling because they need you. Not only to be in the hallways, but [also] to be face-to-face with them, to make contact, and to talk to each one of them. I can't tell you how excited I am about our weekly newsletter. I've always done it. I send it out once a week. We've tried s'mores, and we've tried all different kinds of ways, but the teachers have just told me they just like the old, traditional one. I'd be glad to share it with anyone, but it's a simple template. Normally, it's just a one-pager and on the left-hand side I put the calendar and then little messages about who's got duty that week, just keep it simple. Well, around the third or fourth week, I think I got it from one of the groups that I'm on, but another principal mentioned they were doing an anonymous survey with the teachers where they can add comments about how they are feeling. I said, "You know what? I'm gonna do that. I'm going to put it into my newsletter, anonymously." I made it super simple with glows and grows, and I asked them [teachers] to tell us what we're doing well and to tell us what we could help [with]. Well, about four weeks, three or four weeks ago, I had a teacher that responded, and it was the most painful message I've ever read, because she wrote many "I feel" sentiments:*

> *I feel like I'm not capable. I feel tired.*
> *I feel like I'm not getting anywhere.*
> *I feel like I'm not being listened to.*
> *I feel like I can't get my head above water.*

This really made me think about things, so I called the counseling department. They put me in touch with [a] family treatment center that usually works with families. They sent a team over my campus, and they just did a simple 45-minute self-care session during [teacher] conference periods. They played self-care bingo and other games just to remind teachers to do what they enjoy doing and to ask them, "When was the last they did it?"

Question 3. What does it mean to be an instructional leader today? Give at least one innovative support that you offer for brand-new teachers or for struggling teachers.

Principal 4. *I think it goes in two areas for me. It's practical things that are practical to be an instructional leader and things that you value and that you believe in. The things that I value and believe in are believing [that] all children can learn. That's the number 1. Supporting all students to be the best that they can be and advocating for them at every moment of the day, never letting anybody say the student can't do it. You always have to say, "No, they can, and they will learn, and I'm here to make sure that they do." We offer a lot of support and guidance to our teachers. We also want to make sure that we're informed as leaders, because sometimes we might feel that we know what they need, but then when you do a survey with teachers, you come back to it and you're like, "Whoa." So we always try to make sure that we send out surveys to also get a feel for what they feel that they need, and we provide a lot of support to our teachers. As an instructional leader, you don't have to be good at everything, but you need to know a little bit about everything and you need to be able to go and say, "You know what? I'm going to get the resource for this teacher, or I'm going to get this instructional coach to come in and support this teacher that needs this support." So you must be an observant principal that goes in with the right intention of helping the teacher to be better. Something innovative that we've done for the past years, except when the pandemic came, was to have a choir teacher. My choir teacher takes three classes at a time with support from substitutes, and my teachers go and plan on learning targets for 30 minutes. Then when she does music, my teachers can go for 30 minutes to observe any classes that they want. This helps our teachers that are new teachers, and it helps our veteran teachers to see our new teachers, and so we have now created a culture of respect. A culture of trust in our school. This has really built [a] community in our school.*

Principal 3. *For everyone to get out there and kind of learn from each other and check to see where the campus is. We do peer-to-peer, and that's for, of course, new teachers and for teachers that may need some support. Most of the times, it [the request to observe others] comes from them [teachers]. They want to go observe because of the instructional rounds they get into the classrooms. So that's a great way to kind of learn from each other and have those conversations about what's working in the classroom.*

Question 4. How do you support your staff, particularly your staff of color, to ensure that they feel seen and heard?

Principal 6. *Well, when you talk about supporting your staff, the word has already come up tonight, and it really is about relationships. It is important that we're building strong relationships with our staff. So I take time out to learn the family dynamic of all my staff members so I can talk to them about, "Well, how's your daughter doing?" or "How's your daughter that's in college?" So that whole issue of relationships is key. We do something that we call grand conversation, and we have been utilizing books that talk a lot about respecting diversity and being proud of who you are. We've done green conversations with a book on [diversity]. A very interesting book. It really talks about being accepted by people that do not necessarily look like you. We've done that with our professional staff and with our support staff. One of the things that I'm actually really proud of is that my school has the absolute most diverse teaching staff of any school in the district,*

and that's intentional, because when you have a student popu-
lation that is 50% African American, 22% Hispanic, about 18%
Caucasian, 5–6% two or more races, and 5% Asian students,
your teaching staff needs to mirror the student population as
much as possible. We have a large staff. A good percentage of
African American teachers. The hardest thing I cannot find on
the East Coast are Hispanic educators. I think, probably more
of an East Coast issue, but I value every voice in that building
no matter what you look like. All my teachers of color realize
they can come to me. They can go to my assistant principal, who
happens to be from Bermuda, so we have diversity in adminis-
tration. There's diversity at every level, and we make sure that
everyone feels valued and heard and that everyone in that build-
ing, regardless of position, knows that they have a clear voice and
a voice that is heard and responded to.

Principal 5. *I'd like to piggyback on that. It's very true. She*
mentioned earlier that equity is the center. You got to have equity
in all that [you] do for [your] students, and it's important for
students to see someone that looks like them. Leading those posi-
tions as teacher or administrator or whatever that leadership
role is, it's very important for our students of color to see that,
so that they could emulate and want to emulate the role models
that they see who look like them.

Question 5. Why do you think there is tension between district schools and charter schools? How do we debunk these myths?

Principal 2. *You know, we have to kind of look at how the char-*
ter movement even started when we talk about this question. So
for me, something that I've always learned is the history of the
Smaller Schools Movement right in Chicago, where community
members and teachers wanted to have more say. They wanted to
be more empowered to run the school since they had that expe-
rience of working on the ground, and what we found was that
we had this Smaller Schools Movement. What happened was,
oftentimes, running these schools, unfortunately, it's also a busi-
ness. When community members and teachers didn't always
have the experience with the business end of running schools,
there became a lot of challenges. Next, what you see then was an
opportunity. I don't want to be just sounding like I'm throwing

terms here, but with the neoliberal movement, folks were finding an opportunity to privatize public sectors. So in education, it then became known as this instead of the one spirit that was initially asking, How can community members and how can teachers have more power in running the schools? With a neoliberal movement, a lot of other private industries found opportunities to privatize education, and so this dynamic was at play where we hear about charter management organizations, but we also hear about independent charter schools that are run by community folks and teachers. We see that tension right [between the two types of charters], but often when we hear about the charter movement, that whole history about community activism gets mixed into some of these other politics that we see at hand. What we see here is that challenge when we're talking about the challenge between charter schools and public schools, and then there's also a very real issue. I went to these big public schools. I'm an inner-city kid. I went through them all, and let's be honest, I mean some of these massive schools have absolutely failed communities, oftentimes impoverished communities of color. What we also see is that there are huge bureaucracies of big districts. How does change come in these big districts and in these big schools where there's a lot of bureaucracy and a lot of red tape? What we see with the charter movement is that because it's run in these smaller settings, it gives these opportunities for charters to create other opportunities for community members, and oftentimes, that's real. I work in a charter school, and I have parents say to me, "I don't want my kid to go to that big school, because I went to that school, and a lot of the violence in the community, I see it there, and I experienced it myself." Often, parents want other opportunities and other spaces for their children. That's when we see some of that tension, but it is complex. In terms of what are the myths and what do we do about it, well, that's definitely a challenge.

Question 6. What is your perspective on critical race theory? What's your understanding?

Principal 2. *I just thought of another thing in terms of the public schools and charter schools. When we talk about house school budgets, it is based on attendance, and so there's that "These are my students" thinking. That becomes very real.*

I just want to recognize that as a very real thing when we talk about public education. Where these dollars are going and how we adequately serve our students. There's different positives and challenges within different school settings, and it's very complex. I just wanted to add that regarding the previous question.

In terms of critical race theory, I mean props and love to Kimberly Crenshaw and Sean Bell. These legal scholars that were really drawing from this critical theory [are] really looking at structures. They are looking at how history is not a historical history. It isn't something that you can look up as a fact. History is created. There are narratives, and people come from different perspectives to tell these narratives, and that's the crux of the critical race theory. That critical piece focuses on how we can look and examine systems, not just individuals, and not interpersonal interactions, but how . . . we really look at these systems and how . . . we look at them with a critical lens. How we look at our history is complicated. Who are the actors? Who are the decision makers? We have legal scholars that were looking at how . . . that [plays] out in our policies. Critical race theory initially started as a framework. It was a way to examine policy and started to question how racism is systemically incorporated and implemented in our policies and in our laws. When we talk about the critical race theory movement that we're seeing in schools, it's not about making any particular group feel bad, but it's about coming to terms with the truth. We can't change our society if we don't come to and face the truth of who created decisions in United States and who was able to write the Constitution and who was able to be in those space and in those meetings and from what perspectives and for whose interests. Critical race theory is that opportunity to help us examine very critically why . . . these things [are] happening, but also recognizing that we have power with a critical lens. We have the power to change. People have the power to create these things, and well, people have the power to change these things. So for me and my stance, critical race theory is that opportunity for us to change history, but we have to know it first and we have to know how it's not just an interpersonal thing but . . . also a systemic thing. How do we tease those complexities, and how do we allow our students [to] show that they have the intellectual abilities to think critically and examine things critically to change their own settings? How can they move into the workforce to be able to transform the things that we're doing in our world?

Question 7. What would you say is the most important thing to do year 1 of being a principal?

Principal 1. *I would begin by first advising any new and upcoming leader to know your worth and never settle. That's number 1. Identify your gifts in areas that you desire to further develop. Practice resilience. Regulate your emotions, and commit to being a relentless problem solver. Continue to learn. Remain open-minded. Self-development. I can't say enough about self-development. Fine-tune your skills and leverage them in a variety of areas. Also, connect with like-minded individuals who are already excelling in those areas that you desire to move into. Take risk. Don't play it safe. No one can grow in his or her comfort zone. Demonstrate strength with grace and kindness. Be of service to others and offer support. Then be intentional about self-care, because you cannot pour from an empty glass.*

Principal 5. *I'd like to add to that. Self-care is key. I agree. If you don't take care of yourself, then you can't take care of others. In this role as a principal, we're getting always pulled in so many directions. Everybody counts on us. Everybody needs to talk to us. You got a minute? Teachers need us, parents need us, and students need us, so self-preservation is essential. There's free self-healing, and there's more expensive self-healing. From a bubble bath to a walk with nature to a calm app. To getting your mani and pedi or your facials or your massages to reading [a] juicy novel, whatever it is, self-care is taking care of you first. You must do that. If you don't, then you will not thrive in this role.*

Principal 6. *One thing I would definitely say is that you need to learn your surroundings. You need to learn your staff, and you need to begin creating those relationships.*

Panel Host 1. *I'm even going to take it a step further. When you talk about learning your surroundings, one thing that I always did if I was a new principal in a new community that was not my own community was that I got to know the community. I went to the mom-and-pop shops to introduce myself. I walked around the neighborhood to meet the residents. I remember going up to the gangsters and asking them, like, "Hey, can y'all watch out and make sure that nobody spray-paints the building? Y'all kids go to this school." And they were like, "We got you, miss." If you're blessed and you're fortunate to be able to work in your own community, hats off to you, but if you're not familiar with the community, please get to know the community. Surround yourself with the community.*

Closing Reflection

As you may imagine, this dynamic panel received many accolades for their shared knowledge, wisdom, and experiences. Over 100 attendees joined the live webinar discussion that was held on a late Thursday evening. What was most impressive was that our panelists were strangers prior to this event. What they have most in common, beyond leading schools, is that they lead with truth. Regardless of their perspectives, their philosophies of education, or their years in the profession, all their responses showcased evidence of women who understand their core values and who are committed to embracing their unique identities as assets that cultivate collaborative and effective school cultures. Leading with truth creates freedom. It also creates followers. When teachers, staff members, students, parents, and community members witness authentic confidence from a leader who leads with truth, they will inevitably follow your vision, your ideas, and your heart.

▶ JOURNAL ACTIVITY: NOTE TO SELF

Instructions: Collaboratively work with your leadership team to create a virtual or physical vision board that highlights the elements of the educational paradise you wish to create. Place it where you may refer to it often to celebrate big and small wins of reaching your school climate targets.

REFERENCE LIST

Blankstein, A. M., Houston, P. D., & Cole, R. W. (Eds.). (2010). *Data-enhanced leadership*. The Soul of Educational Leadership Series. Volume 7. Corwin Press.

Mandinach, E. B., & Jackson, S. S. (2012). *Transforming teaching and learning through data driven decision making.* Series 1. Hawker Brownlow Education.

Minty Educational Services. (2021). *Ladies leading legacies webinar.* https://youtu.be/oDVFujTCVtU

Principle

7

Understanding Your Strategy

Learning Outcomes for This Chapter

After reading this chapter, you should be able to:

1. Use data to drive key decisions.
2. Develop, implement, and analyze a strategic plan.
3. Identify inclusive practices for shared decision-making.

Questions to Reflect upon as You Read This Chapter

1. How do teachers connect with each other beyond required meetings?
2. Do you have inclusive practices when selecting strategic planning team members?

I hope that by now, after reading a few chapters of this book, you know that I come to you in peace. My intentions are simply to offer truth as a gift that will help you lead freely while helping you notice practices you may have overlooked or that you're completely oblivious to. After years of peeling back the layers of fakeness, leadership in this new season of my career has never felt better. For starters, I try to love without judgment. I remember my mistakes in life and try not to judge others and their lifestyle choices. Additionally, I don't take myself too seriously. I am confident in knowing that I try my best to do the right

DOI: 10.4324/9781003325635-10

thing, and if I don't meet my goals, then I'll simply try again. I'm also okay with being wrong. With this in mind, here goes another truth about your leadership that you may be completely unaware of, and that is, no one else cares about your organization's strategic goals. There, I said it. And if I were in a room filled with your employees, I would receive some type of confirmation of their shared sentiments through words, laughter, or body language. The reality is that for most of our colleagues, developing strategic goals is a complete waste of time. Oftentimes, leaders develop five-year goals but don't stay in position to witness the maturity of those plans. The next leader takes over with a different vision that overrides the current goals in place. This broken cycle of completion creates a sense of hopelessness and the belief that leaders lack severe "follow-through" on their commitments.

> **"**I'm also okay with being wrong.**"**

If we are reflective in our shared goals for any organization, then we can move towards using strategic plans as roadmaps for transformational change. This reflection first requires us to unpack two major reasons that strategic plans lack relevance to employees. Then we will explore how the three most important stages of strategic planning can be used to drive true organizational change.

▶ TWO REASONS STRATEGIC PLANS LACK RELEVANCE

Reason 1: Leadership and Employee Turnover

According to *Education Week*, Will (2021) uses findings from RAND Cooperation's survey which cited 43% of teachers who left voluntarily before retirement were due to stress and disappointment. In my experience, many of those disappointments occur due to ineffective strategic plans and poor systems management. I can honestly admit that in my first year as founding principal, there were many structures that I built as the year went on simply because they did not exist. However, different from what I'd observed from other school leaders, I decided to lead with truth to offer my staff the opportunity to partner with me for a chance to collaboratively build our educational paradise. This meant that I had to be secure enough in my leadership to identify all the things that we were struggling with as a school community. That's right. Stare my failures right in the face. Read the sticky notes from our community meetings. Hear the testimonials of disappointed parents. Learn about issues that I didn't even know existed. It wasn't easy. Over and over, I had to remind myself not to give excuses. To own it. Why? Because the truth was the foundation to our transformation. Without truth, we would simply be playing schoolhouse instead of developing opportunities for quality learning. Offering our inner-city babies better education mattered to me. It mattered much more than my pride. Looking back on it now, I realized it was the start of my leadership maturity. Valuing the perspectives and funds of knowledge from all members was not only humbling but also opened my eyes to clearly facilitate the process of creating meaningful goals for our school. My growth and openness elevated me to the next level in my leadership career.

One example of this occurring in my leadership journey specifically related to creating a new special education model. Our school was a project-based middle school with a strong enrollment and a strong waiting list. Families in the community wanted us to educate their children. However, like the common story of many charter schools, our special education population grew faster than we expected. Our traditional model included having one Resource Specialist Program (RSP) teacher per grade level who would serve as the case manager and teacher for all students with an individualized education plan (IEP) in their grade level. An essential problem with this model was that our students with special needs would miss out on participating in special projects as their grade-level peers, as well as miss out on attending project-related field trips. For this population of learners, being pulled out of the general education class was dreadful, which ultimately led to extreme behavioral challenges for many of them. The students were unhappy, and the parents were fed up. Something had to be done.

The inevitable happened. We went to litigation for reasons I will not mention. This process helped me learn that litigation should not force change. Real change. Authentic change. Truthful change occurs when leaders take the time to listen and respond to the genuine cares of the people. The epiphany led to the development of a community conversation about the changes that our school needed to adopt in an effort to support our most vulnerable student population. We looked at student data. We listened to the stories from parents and students about their experiences with our special education program. We examined our budget to identify ways we could add more staff, more training, and more resources. Collaboratively, our learning community developed, implemented, observed, and examined our new special education program. The strategy for change was a community effort.

After many sticky notes, emails, meetings, and expert opinions, we hired an outside consultant to analyze, observe, and provide a recommendation for the best special education model for our school. It was imperative for this consultant to consider the community work we had already done, as well as provide us with customized feedback that aligned to the specific aspects of our school community, such as building space, student population, program budget, teacher accessibility, professional development, etc. After two weeks of observations, we were ready to receive feedback. We were strongly encouraged to implement a fully inclusive special education model. This model included three RSP teachers, three paraprofessionals, a program director, a part-time psychologist, external service contracts, and professional development on coteaching for all general education teachers. This shift was grand. This shift was new. This shift was needed. But our school was ready. Ready to work hard to implement a strategic plan that we built together as a team. And it worked!

Reason 2: What's in It for Me

One of the primary goals of a strong strategic plan is to create systems of success. I often liken schools to the animal kingdom. All the members are primarily considered with their habitat and their resources for survival. I desired something different from my school. I desired to display the intersections between our collective and individual goals. The truth is that I knew how

I wanted to lead the team, but I didn't know how to get us there. It wasn't until I stumbled upon a session at a professional conference that I would begin to see the light.

I believe that building genuine relationships is the foundation for sustainable change. During our special education program transition, our school also changed our Special Education Local Plan Area (SELPA). The new SELPA provider hosted an annual meetup that I was invited to attend. I thought it would be a good idea to familiarize myself with local schools and the SELPA staff, so I decided to go. (**SIDENOTE:** I did this often. I took time to attend conferences, seminars, and other scholarly events to prioritize my own leadership development. This meant that I had to develop leaders on campus that I could trust to maintain the daily functionality of our campus. It took time and intentional training, but it was well worth it.) During conference breakouts, I usually jump from session to session to expand my learning reach. I sit in the back so that I can easily leave with minimal distractions. I'm usually successful at this type of maneuvering, but every once in a while, I'll come across a learning session that I do not want to leave. The session on braided initiatives had me glued to my chair.

Braided initiatives is an approach to understanding the intersections between multiple sectors of an institution. It helps with aligning policy and practices across the campus. In other words, it is developing a strategic plan that carefully examines how a school community can double their impact within their capacity. Common solutions from implementing the braided initiative approach results in shared funding, collaborative partnerships, parallel program structures, and common goal setting. For your reference, I have created a sample braided initiative model that includes six school initiatives. The best way to familiarize yourself with the tool is to (1) review the model several times, (2) analyze the purpose for using the model, and (3) replicate the model for your school. Use the braided initiatives template after your team has developed your school's strategic plan.

ACTIVITY #8:
BRAIDED INITIATIVES

Part I: Identify 5–6 Minor Builds

Step 1: Identify the minor builds (school-wide initiatives) that you
will closely monitor this school year.

Step 2: Identify the supports and strategies you will implement for
each minor build per each tier level of student intervention.

	Minor 1 Clinic/SST	Minor 2 Inclusion	Minor 3 Student-Centered Coaching	Minor 4 ELD	Minor 5 PBIS	Minor 6 School Culture
	Freckle Intervention					
Tier 3	Progress Monitoring					
(Individual)	Initial SST Meeting					
	Freckle Intervention					
Tier 2	Clinic Group Support					
(Small Group)	Progress Monitoring					
	Diagnostic Assessment					
Tier 1	Student Survey					
(Whole Group)	Teacher Placement					

Part II: Delegate Shared Leadership

Step 1: Identify which teams or key stakeholder groups will monitor the growth of each minor build.

Step 2: Have each leadership group identify their leader, purpose,
and data collection frequency.

Team	Lead	Purpose	Minor Build	Frequency	Tier Function
Instructional Leadership Team and Student Services Team	Principal/ Assistant Principal	The instructional leadership team and the student services team will support administration with PD planning, reviewing benchmark assessments, and gradebook analysis.	ELD + Inclusion	Weekly	Tier 1 + Tier 2
D-League	Dean of Student Culture		PBIS	Weekly	
ACE Team	Lead Counselor		School Culture	Weekly	
Team Leaders	Lead Team Leader Member		Clinic/ SST	Bimonthly	
Instructional Coaches	Principal		Student Centered Coaching	Bimonthly	

Part III: Identify Tools for Monitoring Student Achievement

Step 1: Have each leadership group identify the tools they will use for data collection.

Step 2: Have each leadership group identify the major stakeholders that will support the success of their minor build.

Minor Build	Area of Focus	Parent Engagement	Student Engagement	Leadership Support	Student Support	Classroom Support	Classified Support
Clinic	Grades + Annual Assessments	Weekly Progress Reports + Parent Conferences	Progress Monitoring (Advisory + College Readiness)	Team Leaders	Lead Counselor	Professional Learning	Monthly Training
Inclusion							
Student-Centered Coaching							
ELD							
PBIS							
School Culture							

▶ THREE STAGES OF STRATEGIC PLANNING

Stage 1: Development

The first stage of a successful strategic planning process is development. During this phase, you analyze school data to identify key areas of concern. Before diving into the process, it is imperative to select the stakeholders that will contribute to creating the plan. One strategy is to develop a criteria or rubric for selecting the individuals on the team to ensure that you have diverse representation. The rubric may entail categories, like (1) stakeholder group, (2) years involved at school, (3) availability, (4) education/professional background, and (5) purpose for participation. These are only suggestions. You may want to vet your criteria with other colleagues to ensure your selection criteria yields diverse, committed, and goal-driven members that represent all major campus stakeholder groups (students, teachers, staff, family, and community). Another strategy could be to provide an open invitation with flexible dates and times for students, parents, and community members to participate. These town hall gatherings should be in multiple locations during considerable hours to ensure that you are intentional about inclusive participation. This strategy typically starts off with large participation, but by the third or fourth meeting, it drops down to the folks who are most available, vested, and committed to keep coming. Whichever method you decide to use to gather your strategic planning team, you must be clear on the intended goals and establish shared norms that will guide the team and keep everyone grounded during episodes of critical conversations. The absence of anchoring communication and participation expectations could ultimately lead to collaborative tension.

After a team of supportive and committed individuals has been established, it's time to let the data ride shotgun. Take time to celebrate your strategic planning team (SPT). The amount of time, energy, and intellectual deposits they will contribute to the school is commendable, so make sure they receive your affirmations on multiple occasions throughout the process. For many school leaders, this requires truth and transparency. Data analysis will reveal your school's strengths and your school's areas of improvement. The SPT members will ask heavy questions. Some may even communicate their concern and advocacy for a particular group of marginalized learners. Leaders, I strongly encourage you to read the next few lines carefully. This is not the time to get defensive. This is not the time to shift the blame. This is not the time to take it personally. This is not the time to minimize group members' concerns. You are a leader, and leading with truth requires you to own it, to name it, and to develop a plan to change it.

> 66 Creating systems of change requires work. 99

▶ STRATEGIC PLAN CASE STUDY

During a strategic planning meeting, committee members noticed the school data revealed that 65% of student dropouts were low-income English-language learners. One parent voiced her concerns and asked, "Why is the school allowing this particular group of students to fall in the cracks?" Before responding to the question, the school principal acknowledged the significance of the data and asked everyone to participate in a quiet moment of reflection and empathy for the many students the school was not able to successfully support to earn a high school diploma. Leading with truth allowed this principal to lead conversations of intimacy and intentionality with committee members. The committee successfully created and implemented a plan that reduced the dropout rate to 20% the following year for the same subgroup of learners.

Creating systems of change requires work. Developing vision does not occur overnight and requires much patience. Strategy is not a race. Strategy is not a one-size-fits-all occurrence. There are a variety of ways for teams to create ideas that are unique to their school goals. The two ways that are most used are research/information gathering and experimentation. As a transformational leader, I have used both methods and successfully reached the intended outcomes. We will explore examples of when and how to select the best method for developing your strategic goals.

Research/Information Gathering. In this process, SPT members identify schools with similar student demographic and populations to explore ways they have successfully championed similar challenges. Gathering data is the first step in articulating if a school has successfully managed to reach certain student achievement goals. Keep in mind that collecting data alone can be misleading and oftentimes does not communicate the full story. For example, school data for one school could reflect 90% of their high school seniors are accepted to college. However, the data does not communicate the exact number of students in the graduating class and does not specifically indicate if those colleges are two-year community colleges or four-year universities. This leads to the next step in research/information gathering, which is networking and visiting campuses.

Education is one industry where stealing is permitted. The power of networking has allowed me to leverage ideas and partnerships from other school leaders that I highly respect. I have learned how to celebrate the success of others and humble myself enough to ask for support so that I may have similar outcomes of success for my learners. An example of this is when I decided to build a high school that would be rooted in projected-based learning (PBL) curriculum and assessment. Although I was familiar with developing PBL content from my previous years of classroom teaching, I understood that it was not my area of expertise, a.k.a. zone of genius. I remember a former colleague raving about a school she had visited in San Diego, California, that had an impressive project-based learning school model. So I reached out to the school to discuss my teaching and learning goals and to ask for their help. Without hesitation, they invited my entire staff to shadow their campus for a week of observation and curriculum development. That year, our teaching staff created some of the most innovative social justice projects I have ever witnessed. Our student completion rates were remarkably high, and parents were extremely impressed with the work their children showcased during exhibition nights.

Experimentation. In this process, SPT members start from scratch to collectively develop solutions that are customized for their school. This approach can take a long time to complete, but in the end, it builds trust and buy-in with all members on the team. Buy-in from SPT members is key during the implementation stage, which we will address next. While there are a variety of ways to facilitate collaborative strategies, one of the tools I have found very helpful is the solution map protocol.

The first process of the solution map protocol is to identify a problem. This problem can already be discovered by the team through data review or common feedback reports from stakeholder members. The SPT must determine if the problem is a high-, medium-, or low-priority challenge. Developing a rubric before is useful to assess the impact of immediate resolve or addressing it another time. All in all, the team must be unified in communicating why this problem was chosen over other challenges.

The next process is to determine the root cause of the problem. This can be done in conversation after everyone has been given a chance to journal their thoughts. Sharing ideas and perspectives is key to understanding everyone's position on the matter. SPT members must be reminded they represent their stakeholder groups and should report concerns, questions, and ideas on behalf of the group at large. It is important to time this segment and ask for everyone to share equity of voice. Timers help keep everyone on track and focused.

The third process in the solution mapping process is to distribute three to four sticky notes to each member to have them

Offers	Communication	Inclusion	Achievement
• Give parents incentives • Raffle prizes for parents with high student engagement • Give parent awards for most engagement • Identify "parent of the month" that has increased parent engagement	• Newsletters • Weekly voice messages • Offer different methods for working parents to get involved with school community • Remind parents about school events using multiple communication methods	• Invite parents to showcase their professional skills and talents • Seek parent feedback for research projects and field trip ideas • Ask parents to co-sponsor clubs/sports with teachers • Allow parents to join school based committees	• Offer parent classes to help deepen their understanding of assignment expectations • Encourage parents to facilitate and host study groups • Give parents documents that clearly articulate the strengths and growth areas for their children

Problem Question
How Do We Increase Parent Engagement?

FIGURE 7.1 Solution mapping tool.

brainstorm solutions to the root cause of the problem. After recording one solution per sticky note, members are to post their ideas on a large board and common space. Again, use a timer to help facilitate transitions and to keep collaboration flowing. Once everyone has posted their responses, the SPT must work as a team to group the common ideas. One of my favorite ways of doing this is by using symbols. For example, draw a moon symbol on a sticky note and then place one sticky note under the moon symbol that represents an idea. Then the SPT must review all the other sticky notes and add common ideas, words, or themes under the moon symbol sticky. Next, draw a circle, a diamond, a star, etc. until all sticky notes have been placed under a symbol. From here, the SPT can identify the symbol with the highest response to initiate further discussions on how to backwards-plan actionable steps towards reaching solutions for this area of need.

Stage 2: Implementation

Now that your solution map has been developed, it's time for the team to decide which initiatives and strategies they would like to implement and how. This process is critical and should not be rushed. The best experiences occur when the team pauses their work to seek feedback from other stakeholder members that are not directly involved on the strategic planning team. This pause could be a onetime invitation for specific guests to attend the next collaborative session. If this is your SPT's selection, be sure to send thorough communication to invitees that outlines the purpose, the goals, and their specific role of contribution for the meeting. This should be reinforced at the beginning of the meeting, as well as an introduction to the team's collaboration norms, to ensure the intended outcomes are met. Another pause option could be a survey distribution to specific members to collect quantitative data on how others rate the categories the team has developed. The communication for this option can also be sent electronically with a deadline for completion. Offering incentives is a great way to increase participation in a timely manner. If selecting this option, be sure that your survey tool only allows for participants to contribute once to prevent your data from being skewed. Once your team has successfully collected inclusive data, it's time to unpause the strategic planning process and move to the next step.

Data analysis is helpful but can also be tricky. Data results are so unpredictable and may sometimes lead to reassessing your initial ideas. For some, this can be a very discouraging stage in the planning process, but it's very important. Developing plans without feedback will most likely result in minimal buy-in and low sustainability. If the data yields a restart, it's better to do it sooner rather than later. In other cases, the data results can help the team further their development of a strong plan. In this scenario, interpreting the data is key. If your data includes interview responses, anecdotes, or open-ended reflections, then your team will need to identify recurring themes and patterns that were communicated directly from the sources. Don't be intimidated by time commitment. This type of research investigation can be fun and rewarding while working with your team. The themes could match the solutions you have already identified or lead to unidentified suggestions. If your data includes percentages and scales, then you will be able to quickly identify alignment between the data and your solutions. Since survey tools are anonymous, you may consider asking questions that will identify the stakeholder's role on campus. Understanding the dominant stakeholder subgroup from the completed surveys could help the team consider the pros and cons of the data responses when deciding on which direction to move towards.

Once the SPT has a unified agreement on the major initiatives and the targeted solutions, it's time to map out the implementation plan. It's important to keep in mind that plans are just plans. When offering services to humans, the outcomes will vary based on a collection of indicators per the individuals you serve. Implementation plans will vary between schools in the same district, they will vary between teachers on the same campus, and they may even vary between children living in the same household. With this in mind, it's a good idea to start with a probable impact number. The probable impact number is the targeted outcome your team aims to reach. It's important to make it a probable and achievable target. This is a "lead with a truth" moment. Find the sweet spot between the historical data of your organization, related to your areas of focus, and the potential outcome of the organization. For example, if the historical data of your organization showcases that parent engagement has always averaged 63% annually but you have recently hired a sharp, new parent engagement coordinator and you've had meetings with several committed parent leaders, then your potential outcome would set your sweet spot at 68%. Attaining a 5% increase in a single year is achievable growth. While this may not be your mastery target, it will effectively measure the growth and impact of your strategic plan. Truth leaders set their teams up for success that can be measured, celebrated, and replicated. It's also important to determine how the success of your strategic plan will be measured. Strategic measures are tools used to correlate measurable goals to strategic solutions. For example, a solution to increase parent engagement for fifth-grade parents at back-to-school night may include a parent/guardian raffle as an incentive to provide (three) field trip scholarships for the fifth-grade overnight science trip. Your SPT may decide to utilize a survey tool during back-to-school night to capture the number of parent/guardians who attend the back-to-school night event. The survey tool (strategic measure) will help the team identify if the parent incentive (strategic solution) impacted the growth in fifth-grade parent/guardian attendees at the back-to-school night event.

Understanding your bandwidth and key players is the next step of the strategic planning implementation process. Instead of using key player, I'd like to refer to this process as understanding your professional capital. Fullan (2012) ascertains, "professional capital [is] the key to scaling up change efforts from individuals to groups to schools and districts. Professional capital is a function of the interaction of three components: human capital, social capital, and decisional capital." From this perspective, members of the strategic planning team should assess the experiences and assets of different members within the school community to leverage their support with implementing the plan. To help understand what this process looks like in action, I have developed three levels for assessing human capital. Review each of the following level as well as the positive and negative impact for each one. Use this scale to determine the best approach for your team's implementation process.

Level 1: Host a team discussion to nominate school members based on the collective knowledge the team has about each individual nominee.

- PRO: The skill sets of each nominee has been witnessed or made to be known to one or more members of the team, so credibility is established.
- CON: The team's knowledge may be limited and could possibly overlook other valuable members within the learning community.

Level 2: Review staff résumés and/or review yearbooks to identify activities and events they have experience with leading or supporting.

- PRO: Opens up the range of persons to nominate and identifies previous participation the nominee may be willing to commit to supporting again.
- CON: Résumés don't always list all skill sets and experiences, and résumés don't always convey a person's effectiveness.

Level 3: Submit a survey to all stakeholders to gauge interest and experience.

- PRO: Communicates each person's willingness to contribute to the solution and allows them to self-rate the knowledge and experience with the major areas of focus.
- CON: This process can be time-consuming and may solicit more support than needed.

Many leaders have communicated the budget as one of the most challenging aspects of implementing a strategic plan. In fact, it's one of the biggest reasons that most leaders begin with the budget to ensure they don't make false promises to the strategic planning team (SPT) and the general school members. While this practice may appear to be leading with truth, it is not. In our explanation of tangible truth, we addressed how sensory data (money) can often mislead leaders into limiting their options. In some cases, I've even witnessed this level of limitations leading to the development of some of the most pessimistic plans for schools with great potential. Now, please don't misread my posture by thinking I'm suggesting for leaders to be dismissive to their responsibilities as financial managers. During my years as a school leader, I maintained a conservative spending budget and demonstrated exemplar financial management. However, I did not allow finances to overrule passion. If our school community displayed a strong desire to implement solutions that we collectively believed would improve the quality of teaching and learning for our students, then I figured out how to lead us. I wrote grants, sought philanthropic support, established key community partnerships, etc. My truth was that I made up in mind that financial restrictions were never permanent, and if I had the will, then there was always a way to get the job done.

The implementation rollout of the strategic plan requires intentional planning. Calendaring the phases of introducing an initiative to the team requires a comprehensive understanding of planned events. This may be a good place where the SPT members incorporate use of the braided initiatives model to determine how initiatives intersect and to identify possible conflicts of interest. This is also the stage where you want to be sure to include support from the administrative and office staff. Leading with truth recognizes the significant value that members in the office staff carry, especially when scheduling or calendaring school events. The great news about this task is that it could be done in a single meeting session if properly planned and leverages support from highly skilled organizers within the school community. While many may think this process simply entails a backwards plan design, there are other important features to consider. At one of my former schools, we were adopting the project-based learning model on a six-week carousel. This meant teachers were required to launch, teach, assess, and prepare students to present their findings every six weeks. Reflecting on it now makes me shake my head to my own naivete as a school leader. Aside from sending our teachers to a three-day training at an exemplary school model, I can truthfully admit to not having a productive implementation rollout plan. Before rolling out the plan, our team did not consider holidays that would affect the days of instruction in each six-week carousel. At the beginning of the year, we spent a significant amount of time training the students on our paradigm shift, but we did not consider training new students who enrolled mid-year. Our team did not have any parent representatives, so there was lack of consideration on the nights we selected to host student exhibitions. In fact, by the time we prepared for the third six-week carousel, our teaching staff communicated they did not have adequate time to design new projects and simultaneously prepare students for state assessments. At my end-of-year reflection, I recognized that while we were enthused about implementing a new initiative, we faltered in implementing a strategic plan with careful consideration. I would not say the experience was a complete disaster, but I believe all stakeholders would have benefited more if the team had carved out focused time to carefully calendar the rollout plan.

The final piece of the implementation stage is the communication plan. Unfortunately, this piece is usually the least considered but requires the greatest attention. After all, you can't implement something great without informing folks about the five Ws and one H (who, what, where, when, why, and how). As discussed earlier, human connectivity is centered on communication. In Chapter 2 we discussed the various communication preferences according to the generations represented in the organization. Many schools are heavily criticized for lacking communication about events, grade reporting, and disciplinary actions of students. It's unfortunate that the climate of some schools is to act first and explain later. When stakeholder members feel left out of the loop, it creates hostility and lack of trust. Therefore, developing a robust communication plan will offer shared understanding that establishes common ground for school community members to embrace new initiatives. Even good ideas go unnoticed if communication is not delivered adequately. Leading with truth requires school leaders to consider systems and protocols that track how communication is being delivered and who is receiving it. Leaders must consider multigeneration methods of communication (i.e., paper newsletters, emails, text messages, social media, website, etc.). Keep in mind that communication rollouts require ongoing research and analysis. What worked in the past may not work today. This is one of the reasons it's important to become lifelong learners as well as develop positive relationships with members to leverage professional capital to ensure the school's functionality is productive and sustainable.

Communication Rollout Case Study

A new middle school principal decided to host a carnival during back-to-school. The planning committee agreed the best method of communication about the carnival would be to have a three-week social media campaign. Each day, the social media representative of the committee posted school tweets on Twitter, Instagram memes, and Facebook incentives to get the parents enthused about coming to the carnival. On the night of the carnival, an elderly woman pulled the principal aside to inquire why she had not received any information about the carnival. She also mentioned that she was a pillar in the community and, in the past, had proudly served as a community networker to communicate all school-related activities to residents and small business owners. The principal informed the woman that all communication was provided on the school's social media pages. The woman replied with disappointment on her face and simply stated, "I don't own any social media accounts."

Stage 3: Observe and Examine

The observation/examination process is my favorite stage of strategic planning. This is where potential magic happens. This is the moment where your hard work and patience are put to action. In some cases, it is a huge success, but in other cases, the desired outcomes are not always met. In any case, leaders who lead with truth should prepare their teams to observe without bias and examine with honesty. The last thing our schools need is to continue implementing broken practices because of what I like to call innovative attachment. For me, innovative attachment occurs when innovative designers cling to ineffective products because of the emotional connection they've made throughout the development process. Instead of carefully determining the accuracy and efficacy of what their product provides, they'd rather keep it, use it, and praise it simply because it's their brainchild. Can you imagine what would happen if race car engineers behaved this way? There would be a multitude of disastrous crashes, physical injury, facility destruction, and a long list of utter chaos on the racetrack if engineers weren't tasked with observing multiple car examinations before drivers zoomed off their starting line positions.

As a casual Formula 1 (F1) fan, I've become quite amazed by the dynamic qualities of British motor race driver Sir Lewis Hamilton. At age 37, Hamilton holds the record for the most F1 race car wins, totaling 103. More than just a race car genius, Sir Lewis Hamilton prides himself in promoting diversity in his industry by introducing students of color to STEM education. Currently, he is the only black driver in F1's world championship, which began in 1950, and he believes all children of color should learn about the multiple STEM-related jobs available in motor racing. A YouTube video (UBS, 2021) captures Hamilton as he surprises a group of elementary students during their trip to Mercedes AMG Petronas Formula One Headquarters. I sat in pure amazement as he explained to the children that over 200 people participate in the process of designing, racing, observing, and examining one car for one driver. These engineers are aware of the potential danger that exists if the car does not function at its optimum capacity. They're also aware of the danger their negligence may cause to the driver if the proper analysis isn't performed on the car's functionality. Hamilton explained to the children that he trusts his team to be the experts that help him reach the finish line. What a powerful testament! Now, let's imagine that your strategic plan is the race car. It's important for you to critically observe and examine your plan in action to prevent severe damage from happening in classrooms. Learning the pros and cons of your plan may further help your team discover the best course of action for reaching your desired destination. Early warning signals may trigger the need to establish interventions or abort the plan altogether. It's important to embrace the idea that innovation is a process. It takes many trials and errors before it's solid. Understanding this truth sooner than later will prevent your team from experiencing innovative attachment. Leading with truth is vital at this stage of the game. After all, you and your SPT members are the group of experts everyone's trusting to help them reach the finish line.

Start Small

Almost all my program rollouts or new initiatives began small. I strategically selected a pilot group to implement the new idea from start to finish. This helped me in two ways. For starters, it kept the observations manageable. For example, if you're starting a new reading intervention program, begin with one grade level so that it's easy to train and support a sample group of teachers and their scholars. This is not only easy to manage but also easy to budget. The required training services, digital licenses and tools, books, and other necessary equipment for your new initiative are simpler to attain in the pilot phase. Also, in the event it doesn't work in your favor, it's better to communicate a smaller loss for a pilot group than to communicate a larger one for your entire school. During observations of the new program, be sure to select strategic planning team members and nonteam members. This is called the peer review phase. All valid research is vetted through peer review and/or institutional review boards (IRB). The purpose of this process is to ensure that research tools and protocols are appropriately in place to protect the welfare of human subjects. It is wise to treat your strategic plan initiatives as research involving the minds, behaviors, and emotions of our most vulnerable humans, our children. Conducting a formal peer review process will validate the reason for adopting new practices on your campus. When this process is skipped, avoided, or even minimized to external campus stakeholders (i.e., district-level leaders), it creates the risks of lack of buy-in from the end users (campus teachers and staff) who are charged with offering the service to students and their families. Now, once you've assembled your observation team(s), it's time to prepare them. For calibration purposes, be sure that your SPT develops rubrics that are holistic, with a checklist. Holistic rubrics communicate specific outcomes and provide observational examples. For instance, a holistic rubric for student engagement may identify that an observational outcome for students is to express their thinking. It will provide the user with examples of student expression, such as speaking, writing, drawing, and other nonverbal actions. A checklist is a simple reference for novice observers to gain quick information and direct understanding of the observational expectations. It's always a good idea to facilitate a training for observers to streamline the process. Now, the second reason it's good to pilot a new initiative is to gain buy-in from teacher practitioners. If your plan or new adoption is a success, the sample teacher group will be strong influencers for their peers. In most instances, their affirmations and experiences make them credible for their peers to accept the new changes. The truth is that educators are more willing to embrace change that's celebrated and led by their colleagues. Expand your professional capitol by offering the sample teachers the chance to practice their leadership and facilitation skills to train and support the next group of program adopters. Ultimately, this becomes a win for everyone!

More Than Once

The more data, the more guidance you'll have when you are finalizing your decisions and/or adjusting your strategic plan. Of course, this requires intentionality and proper planning. Leading with truth requires you to frequently assess your bandwidth and pass the ball if you don't have the capacity to sustain consistency. For example, if every Thursday for the next three weeks the SPT has decided to facilitate training for observers, conduct the observations, and examine the results, it's best to lead with truth to determine if you have time to fully participate and engage in the process. It's okay to trust your SPT members. It's okay if someone else on the SPT is the leader of the team. It doesn't diminish your position or contributions. In fact, a truth reflection will allow you to avoid becoming a distraction in a process that requires a level of strong replication to produce accurate data. However, I understand passion, and if you're passionate about participating in the observation/examination stage, be sure to agree on the frequency of your observations and schedule blocks of uninterrupted time for thorough examinations of your observational data. Student samples, teacher samples, times of day, day of the week, weather forecast, observer roles, campus events, deadlines, budget, etc. are all major contributing assets or liabilities when collecting observable data. Accurate data matters, so make it count.

Experts in the Room

Let me be clear with what I'm about to say. Leading with truth does not promote exclusive practices rooted in ostracizing people from participating in a collective decision-making processes. The core of my career in education has focused on social justice leadership in classroom spaces and beyond. Observation and data collection are of many processes that everyone is welcomed to participate in. Why? Because we value the multiple perspectives that a collection of school community members bring to the table. We understand that this collective gathering of data offers authentic and transparent insight to the practices, problems, and potential of what's currently happening on the campus. However, as you continue your journey of strategic planning, it's critical to only have your most competent and knowledgeable stakeholders examine and interpret the data. In this "lead with truth" moment, it is wise to keep the goal in mind. A goal in this stage is to determine if the strategic plan is effective. Another goal is to synthesize data to help determine the next steps for your SPT members. A final goal is to understand how your plan impacts the way in which children learn, teachers teach, and community members collaborate.

For those of you who disagree, let me offer an analogy for your consideration of agreement. When I was aged 10, my father remarried my bonus mom, who I affectionately call Mama Donna. When Mama Donna was an adolescent, she suffered a major injury resulting in permanent visual impairment of her left eye. She wears contact lenses in the day, and in the evening, she wears glasses to support her vision. The optometrist has informed my parents to expect that one day she'll lose vision in both eyes since the right eye muscles are working twice their capacity to provide her with eyesight. As children, we have shared responsibilities in driving at night, reading bills or emails, and other visual-related supports to help our mom. Her comfort has been one of our family's priorities, especially if we desire to indulge in her delicious homemade Southern cuisines. Since her eye sustainability is critical, she is required to have frequent eye exams so that we are aware of the current conditions of her eye strength. We have developed confidence in the expert training and knowledge of the optometrist to review the observations of her visual capabilities and provide an accurate analysis of her eye performance. The analysis review serves as the leading catalyst for determining the best care for Mama Donna's vision sustainability. Prohibiting non-experts in this process is not an exclusive practice but rather a very wise one.

Selecting expert participants should be determined on the goals of the strategic plan. The participants should not be restricted to on-campus stakeholders, but you may want to consider participants who possess FERPA rights to access student and teacher records. For example, if your strategic plan aims to increase student attendance for English-language learners, then you may select the organization's director of ELD to participate in the examination and analysis process. Their skills, training, and knowledge of network-wide data could offer significant insight to understanding your data. Additionally, your expert team does not have to be large. A team of three to five participants will suffice, especially if you have limited time to coordinate everyone's schedules for a lengthy meeting. I recommend setting aside a full day at an off-campus location to ensure that your time together is uninterrupted. Data analysis requires critical thinking and deep dialogue exchange. Participants should be free to share, free to question, free to disagree, and free to think quietly. In my experience, this has worked best when I've sent my data analysis participants away to an off-campus meeting room that I've rented for a day from a nonprofit, museum, or hotel banquet hall. The experience is always greatly appreciated and has always resulted in highly intriguing data reports. I have always made clear the purpose and expectations of the participants' gathering. In most cases, the expectations include a detailed graphic report and an electronic presentation. In full transparency, I ask them to make it dummy-proof because I am the dummy. Leading with truth allows you to recognize the areas that require you to leverage support from other professional experts in your school community. It also allows you to ask for the information to be communicated in the most simplistic form to build your confidence as you prepare to share the data with others. Demonstrating vulnerability is key to leading with truth.

More Than One Way to Win

I wouldn't feel comfortable leaving you hanging without addressing the elephant in the room. What if the results of my strategic plan do not impact student growth? I know it may possibly become a burning question for you, because it was always one for me. I can truthfully admit to having experiences with innovative attachment to programs and curriculums that I had designed with other colleagues. I can also admit to losing hope when all the effort, time, conversations, feedback, observations, and thorough examinations of those initiatives did not move the needle forward with our summative student data results. In one example, I was purely exhausted, I felt defeated, and I feared humiliation. During these moments, I typically look for wise counsel from my trusted village of family and close friends, but this time, I simply needed my dad.

It was the end of the year, and we had just revealed the student outcome data from a PBIS (positive behavior intervention and supports) intervention my SPT developed, launched, and piloted for a full year on my campus. Our target goal was to decrease office referrals for a sample population of black and brown fifth-grade boys. The SPT developed a plan that entailed the following: (1) careful review of three years of office referral data, (2) fifth-grade teacher interviews, (3) PBIS training for fifth-grade teachers, (4) hosting multiple parent meetings, (5) purchasing pilot subscription of parent square, (5) student incentives, and (6) social-emotional supports for our sample population. Additionally, we partnered with outside agencies who provided male mentorship courses and sponsored field trips. The SPT strategically decided to provide these services to all fifth-grade boys and teachers to collect comparison data. Although we monitored our progress throughout the year, the summative data still reported disproportionate numbers in our office referrals for our sample population. It was late spring, and we had just finished hosting a town hall meeting to reveal our results. The attendance of external stakeholders was low, but most teachers and staff stayed after to ask a long list of questions I dreaded answering. I answered truthfully and even honestly admitted to feeling defeated. I remember walking to my car thinking that I wanted a hug from Dad. I knew I could find him either at church or at the bowling alley. I didn't call or text to see where he was located. I just found my car drifting towards the bowling alley, where his truck was conveniently parked in its usual spot. I got out quickly and felt relieved when he greeted me with an enthusiastic, surprised look on his face. It felt good to feel his embrace.

My father is extremely competitive. He doesn't like to lose. He values beating his own scores and will spend a fair amount of time practicing until he accomplishes his goals. He is the family GOAT, a.k.a. the guy everyone wants to beat at cards, dominoes, checkers, pool, bowling, etc. This also means that he doesn't like to be disturbed when he's in his zone. Knowing this, I looked up at the televised scorecard and then down at him as he perfected his stance before releasing the ball to hit another strike. It was impressive. I sat thinking that maybe it was a bad idea to come here to dump my troubles on him during his pastime activity. After all, he deserved it after 30 years serving as a high-rise carpenter/foreman throughout Southern California. I tried to discreetly excuse myself so that he could stay in his zone, but like most parents, he knew something was up. He didn't let me leave. Instead, he rented me some shoes and said, "Whatever it is, take it out on the pins." I stopped lacing up my shoes and looked down the lane at the ten shiny white-and-red bowling pins and thought to myself, *You ain't said nothing but a word, game on!*

I am competitive like my dad, but my athletic skills are not the best. My dad and six brothers are naturally gifted with hand-and-foot coordination plus speed and strength. They've always teased me when I was younger by taunting me and saying, "You must have only got a double scoop of brains." And while this may be true, I still don't like to lose. So there I was, getting frustrated that I wasn't striking the pins like my dad. I tried to learn from his quick, on-the-spot tutorial on how to stand and on how to roll and release, but it wasn't working. In this moment, I felt like I was getting a double scoop of defeat. I was trying to hold back my tears because I hate crying in front of my dad, but it was too late. And in his typical fatherly way, he didn't budge to my emotions. Instead, he kept bowling and finally uttered these words of gold: "There is always more than one way to win." And just like that, I remembered that I bowl best when I roll a straight, underhanded release. Yes, you've guessed it. Two hands on the ball, knees bent, legs apart, start from the middle, and release the ball as fast and as hard as I can. It's not the best method. Far from professional. Not recommended. But at least I got my STRIKE!

That night, I drafted an email to go out to all community stakeholders, inviting them to attend an impromptu town hall do-over meeting. I expressed my sincere apologies and asked them to give me another chance to present our student data from our PBIS initiative. This was a huge "lead with truth" moment. I was excited and nervous at the same time. I was taking a risk of being mocked or dismissed, but I knew it had to be done. After scheduling the email to go out at the start of the next day, I stayed up through the early morning preparing for my do-over presentation. I creatively used bowling as my theme, and I was proud of the outcomes. Saturday could not have arrived any sooner.

Finally, Saturday morning greeted me. I woke up early to shower and to get dressed. I wore my power color, red, for self-affirmation and confidence. I jetted out the door to stop by the grocery store to pick up light refreshments and flowers for the sign-in table. I was so thankful that members of the SPT agreed to support me with setup and cleanup duties. They were as clueless as everyone else was, but they trusted me and agreed to follow my lead. Their support spoke volumes to me in this moment. I was surprised to see that we had a larger turnout than before, and of course, district leaders were in the room. It was 9:00 a.m. sharp, so I grabbed the mic like it was that bowling ball and released the most unorthodox student data presentation of my career. I started off by holding printed copies of the numerical office referral data that I presented two days prior. Then, I grabbed a lighter and I burned it. Now, don't get too nervous. I made sure to properly plan my crazy actions with my campus maintenance crew to ensure safety was maintained. My focus was to emphasize the importance of creating a campus culture that used data-informed practices to drive change. I used the next moments to present to the audience ten ways the PBIS initiative yielded positive data that was overlooked because of my narrow focus. I referenced the ten pins of bowling to cite the various ways our students were impacted academically, socially, and developmentally. I showed evidence from our community mentor meetings, field trips, and teacher trainings as claims of success. I invited the fifth-grade boys to share their experiences, and I gave our fifth-grade teachers a chance to discuss their honest reflections. Next, I facilitated a gallery walk activity where all attendees could contribute their ideas on how to improve the intervention for the next year. Participants enjoyed the option of participating digitally with their smartphones or physically by walking to each station. The SPT team quickly synthesized the feedback data, and we showcased the collective ideas that were just developed by our school community. Just as I was about to conclude the meeting, I looked in the far back corner of the room and recognized my handsome dad crossing his arms in the X position as a nonverbal message for the word *ten*. In bowling language, an X represents a STRIKE! It has been one of my most sentimental "lead with truth" moments that will be cherished forever.

▶ JOURNAL ACTIVITY: NOTE TO SELF

Instructions: Start considering how you will select the members of your strategic planning team (SPT). Try not to have preselected members in mind. Instead, re-read the selection methods mentioned in this chapter and decide which one you plan to implement.

REFERENCE LIST

Fullan, M. (2012). *Professional capital: Transforming teaching in every school.* Teachers College Press.

UBS. (2021, October 27). *Welcome to the Hamilton engineering school.* YouTube. https://youtu.be/gdeD2jhu9IU

Will, M. (2021). Teachers are stressed out and it's causing some to quit. *Education Week.* www.edweek.org/teaching-learning/teachers-are-stressed-out-and-its-causing-some-to-quit/2021/02

Part 4
Lead with
True Service

Understanding Your Influence

8

Learning Outcomes for This Chapter

After reading this chapter, you should be able to:

1. Explore the importance of leading beyond your school site.
2. Understand the power of networking.
3. Learn your professional brand.

Questions to Reflect upon as You Read This Chapter

1. How do you partner with other schools, leaders, community leaders?
2. How can your expertise reach people beyond your school site?

Leading any organization is tough work. While purposeful to most, the truth is that leading people consumes your time, energy, and many thoughts. It's the reason many leaders lose their core values in exchange for the many managerial tasks they're required to handle. However, I'd like to pause and take this time to remind you that you are more than a principal. You possess virtue beyond your school's campus, and it's very important that you tap into the many other assets you carry to sustain balance in your career. One of the roles I contributed to

DOI: 10.4324/9781003325635-12

beyond my role as a campus leader was serving as a curriculum developer for our entire charter network. The experience was life-changing and remains one of my most memorable years in education.

> **"**Leading any organization is tough work.**"**

At that time, I served for a multisite charter school network. Six teachers from other campuses and I were asked to join a special taskforce to collaborate on restructuring the design of our curriculum. All teachers at all campuses used the same course design protocol to develop project-based units. We were charged with reflecting on the outcomes we wanted for our learners across the network. In other words, our leadership asked us to dismantle the curriculum and start from scratch. Collectively, we created a unique set of indices that would later be used to help guide all teachers in the network to develop project-based units. We knew that our design would ultimately help young people master content knowledge and skills that empowered student agency in their communities. It was the first time in my career where I felt like I was a part of something meaningful, something that aligned with my philosophical beliefs in education. This was bigger than us. We were part of a movement. We were part of a legacy. The best part was that we were all pure at heart, and we genuinely wanted to develop something great for our babies. The chemistry of the team was so authentic and seamless. We were radical change agents aiming to contribute to a paradigm shift in urban education. These were great times.

Mahatma Gandhi once said, "True beauty lies in the purity of heart." In all honesty, I don't believe we knew how far our work would reach to influence others. We were simply accomplishing the goals we set for ourselves as representatives of our teacher colleagues and advocates for our students. We were not in competition with each other, and we greatly valued the skills and strengths that were shared between us. We met once a week at the central office location after a full day of teaching at our respective campuses. I say *central office location* without fully describing the distance in traffic many of us faced coming and returning home in the late evening. The sacrifice was real, but every person on the team was all in. We were committed. The old saying "Time flies when you're having fun" was true in this case because I honestly cannot remember how long it took for us to complete the very first edition of the manuscript. We started. We stopped. We erased it and started again. We were pleased. We were unpleased. We were stuck. We were motivated. We were stifled. We needed more inspiration. We were stuffed. We were free. We were creating. After the first draft was complete, we invited a few peers in the network to review the manuscript and give feedback. This was nerve-racking because we wanted our hard work to be accepted. We wanted validation. We wanted praise. But we all know that's not always the case when you share your craft with others. The feedback wasn't too bad. The few additions our colleagues suggested were reasonable and fair. But this team was unique. Now that I think about it, we all demonstrated small to large characteristics of a perfectionist. This means that we went back to the drawing board to improve and take the manuscript to the next level. This meant more time. More time. More time.

After the final draft was complete, we were tasked with training the entire teaching staff on the new framework, design, and implementation protocols. This was a heavy lift because it was new. As teachers, we all knew there would be pushback from some of our colleagues, but that didn't intimidate us. In fact, on several occasions, we invited colleagues to give us feedback on our professional training and rollout plan. Some contributed and offered great suggestions, and others gave minimal critique. Overall, the implementation rollout went as planned and an entire network of teachers throughout the state was using our manuscript to design projects for our youth. We started with blank sheets of paper that later became a guide for instructional design. For me, this was mind-blowing.

Then something happened. Like electricity, different members of the team were being tagged to speak at different conferences across the nation about our manuscript. We didn't know it at that time, but we were way ahead of the education landscape with this new material. We even received a few pitches to market and publish the document. For us, this was a hard "no." We didn't see the document as a one-size-fits-all guide to project-based curriculum design. We believed that it was unique to our network, our teachers, and our youth. We were willing to help others do the work of collaborating with their peers to develop their own guides, but that offer was often dismissed. Most felt it was too time-consuming, or they just didn't want to do the "real work," as we often referred to it. My time with the organization was short-lived after the year we developed the manuscript. I decided to return to the local district as a site administrator to support the children in my neighborhood. I didn't know then that my service on the curriculum taskforce would be a major contributing factor to elevating my career and building my reputation as an "expert" project-based instructional leader.

Three years after contributing on the special curriculum project, I was transferred to serve as an administrator for a school that was in the process of adopting an interdisciplinary problem-based curriculum. One of the reasons I was selected to serve at the site was my experience on the project-based curriculum taskforce. In fact, I was able to hire one of my former colleagues to lead professional development with the teachers at my new campus. My new school was successful in the adoption and implementation of the interdisciplinary curriculum model, later receiving notable accolades for their accomplishments. Who would have guessed that a group of radical educators whose ambitions were purely set on being agents of social change would evolve to influencing teachers and districts across the nation? Leading with truth will inevitably establish opportunities that you won't have to sign up to receive. The reputation of true and authentic leaders will overwhelmingly precede them time after time.

In Chapter 1 I reflected on how my mama raised her children to look for opportunities to help other people. In my early twenties, it was clear to me that my service to others would be through helping children. Although I chose a career in education to support the developmental growth of young people, I've always believed there were alternative ways to teach and mentor young people. I knew that I wanted to provide extended wraparound services to our most vulnerable and traumatized youth. On December 30, 2011, I had a vision to develop a nonprofit organization that would provide mentoring, mental health support, community service events, and academic advisory to underserved and underrepresented teenage youth in my community. By March of 2012, Lancaster Youth Developmental Foundation (LYDF) was birthed, and I acquired a strong team of reputable and committed board of trustees who partnered with me to develop and deliver the mission and values of our organization.

I remember the first community event like it was yesterday. We partnered with the city council and the local high school district to offer a mentoring program for young people that would culminate in a community service project for the youth to give back to their neighbors. One week before the service project, we met with youth participants in the park for our Mental Toughness for Success (MTS) mentoring program. The MTS program entailed activities, small-group discussions, and daily reflection that challenged participants to think about their future in the areas of career, service, and good health. Students heard from various career leaders in the community, they learned about healthy eating and daily exercise tips, and they participated in a full day of providing free lawn mowing service to 50 community homes. This program would later become our annual signature launch program for each new cohort of LYDF participants.

After three years of sustainable services, the board and I were looking to strengthen our program and expand our reach to service more young people in the community. We wanted to meet our city mayor to leverage his professional and financial capital. The process was not going to be as easy as we thought, but we were willing to take risks for the opportunity to pitch our program in his office. Leading with truth requires you to believe and hope for the impossible. Some call this out-of-the-box thinking, but our group simply called it faith in action.

Miracles still happen if you believe. Here I was, trying to strategically think of how I was going to acquire a meeting with the city mayor, and without my knowing, I met and became well acquainted with his secretary at a friend's baby shower. The friendly exchange between my new acquaintance and me was so refreshing and uplifting that she offered to schedule me to meet with the city mayor within a week. It all happened so fast that it was hard for me to catch my breath. But it happened. I still remember the celebration moment our team shared with each other when I shared the good news. After one evening of celebration, we quickly gathered ourselves to prepare our pitch deck. We wanted it to be perfect. We needed this moment to take us to the next level.

We arrived on time, which in the business world means that we arrived late. The secretary gave me a hard scowl but quickly gathered our things to set us up to present in the conference room. I completely understood her stance. She had put her name on the line to get us the appointment and did not want us to ruin the golden opportunity. As young black community leaders, we knew that personal meetings with the mayor were not easy to establish. We knew the assignment to represent our community, our students, and our families was a big, big deal. We quickly prayed and prepared to shoot our best shot!

To be honest, I was greatly disappointed when the city manager excused the mayor for his absence. While I understood the reason, I remember feeling defeated but quickly choosing to push through with my best efforts. In the mayor's absence, we were greeted by the rest of the members of the city's cabinet. Once introductions were complete, our presentation began. I started with an overview of our nonprofit organization by highlighting our origin, milestones and community impact. After about three slides, I handed the presentation clicker over to our first board president, who began discussing our vision and future projects that were in the process of development. And boom! That was when the magic happened. The city manager immediately interrupted the presentation. He didn't even apologize for his abrupt interjection but went on to say, "Hold on! Hold on! Hold on! This, by far, is the best presentation pitch I've experienced since my tenure with the city. I don't know what you want, but you automatically get my endorsement. This level of professionalism deserves our support." I can barely remember how the presentation concluded because of the magnitude of that moment. We arrived thinking we wanted one thing, and we departed receiving more than we could have imagined. To this day, LYDF continues to impact the lives of young people in the community through outreach and service in collaboration with city and private sponsors.

▶ BRAND LIKE A BOSS

In the year 2019, I was honored to present at the Association of California School Administrators (ACSA) Women's Leadership

Conference. The title of my presentation was Platinum Platforms for School Leaders: Brand Like a Boss. The objectives of the discussion were to highlight the significance of naming and branding your professional identity. I hoped for audience members to walk away with the motivation and resources necessary to magnify their strengths, talents, wisdom, experiences, wit, and ambitions in a strategic way that would market their greatness. One of the activities I asked them to complete was to fill out a "zone of genius" sheet in three minutes. What we discovered was that many of the highly skilled and professional women participants did not possess the ability to pinpoint their greatness. Ironically, I asked them to do the same task for their direct supervisor or their spouse, and they did so without hesitation. I remember thinking to myself, *This is absurd!*

A few weeks before the presentation, I, too, completed the "zone of genius" activity. Gay Hendricks (2010) describes this about the "zone of genius" in his book *The Big Leap:*

> In this zone, you capitalize on your natural abilities
> which are innate, rather than learned.
> This is the state in which you get into "flow,"
> find ceaseless inspiration, and seem to not only
> come up with work that is distinguished and unique,
> but also, do so in a way that excels far and
> beyond what anyone else is doing.

One thing that I discovered that remains true today is that I have natural gifts in the areas of communication and oratory skills. This is my brand! I am confident that when I open my mouth to speak, ears are automatically drawn to the sound of my words. Over the years, I have practiced developing these natural gifts at every opportunity offered. In many cases, I have spoken or presented at events for free. In other scenarios, I have presented daily or weekly announcements at my school and my church. You see, this practice has led to my permanent stage comfort. Furthermore, my brand now yields paid speaking contracts at various events throughout the world. It is essential to brand your brilliance so that it will make room for your personal and professional successes. What's your zone of genius?

ACTIVITY #9:
ZONE OF GENIUS

Using Hendricks's top three questions, record and reflect on your answers to unlock your brilliance.

Hendricks's Questions	Response	Specific Examples
What work do you do that doesn't seem like work?		
In your work, what produces the highest ratio of abundance and satisfaction to the amount of time spent?		
What is your unique ability?		

▶ JUST SAY YES!

Merriam-Webster defines *yes* as a word to express agreement. In most cases, when we agree to do something, we understand our commitment. On the contrary, a blind yes can be considered as an agreement where we aren't aware of our full commitment. It has been in these moments where my blind yes (or simply faith) has led me to the most rewarding opportunities. The most recent blind yes occurred suddenly. I received a phone call from a very close relative asking me to speak at an event. Apparently, the original keynote speaker was no longer available, and they needed someone to do the job. Before I said yes, the only information that I knew about the commitment was that I would be speaking/motivating children and that it was a virtual event. I wasn't concerned with the ticky-tacky details. I just wanted to be of service for my loved one.

> **❝**My yes was becoming the gateway to my destiny. **❞**

I had less than 48 hours to prepare, so I needed to think quick! I just happened to be in a hotel, visiting the new city I would soon be calling home. My purpose of being in town was to meet with the builders of my new construction property. The timing wasn't the best, but it was helpful to have the quiet space of the nice hotel to think and prepare. Now ironically, I had recently spoke at a teen summit the weekend before. Once again, I met a nice stranger who I now call friend at a beautiful brunch spot in the city. I enjoyed good conversation with him and his wife at the bar since the place was too packed to seat us at our own individual tables. I learned that he was program coordinator for a youth program sponsored by the chamber of commerce, and after learning about my background, he asked me to speak at their upcoming youth summit. And like that, I said yes. Saying yes to speak at the summit gave me tools and content to speak at the virtual youth event. I can't imagine how things would have turned out if I didn't have the materials from the previous speaking engagement. Does that happen to you? Have you ever experienced one occurrence perfectly connecting to another? It gets me super hyped when I witness the intentionality of life.

My presentation at the virtual youth event was a slam! Since it was my second time presenting the content, I was comfortable in my zone. The technical flow of the event was smooth, which is always a plus in virtual settings, and the young attendees interacted and were engaged. I received high praise from all my relatives who attended, so I felt good about my labor of love. Just when I thought it was over, it was just beginning. My yes was becoming the gateway to my destiny.

It only takes one yes for your blessing. Yes to the teen summit. Yes to the virtual youth event. And now, yes to the annual scholarship luncheon. Can you believe it? The president of the organization who sponsored the virtual youth event requested for me to keynote their annual scholarship luncheon. How cool was that? Of course, I said yes, and of course, I nailed it. This time, there were three times as many virtual participants who attended and participated in my presentation. I spoke on a delicate topic that I'm passionate about, so once again, the high energy flowed naturally. And do you want to know what happened next? I received a text by one of the audience members requesting me to speak at a very important event for their school district. By now, you should know that I said yes, and in less than six days, I was on a plane, traveling to speak at another event. The speaking requests continue to evolve, and I'm continually honored by each opportunity. So I say, put a yes in your spirit so that it can easily flow from your lips. Your first yes may lead to your greatest destiny.

▶ JOURNAL ACTIVITY: NOTE TO SELF

Instructions: Unlock your full potential. Identify your zone of genius. Next, think of your brand, and identify two opportunities that will receive your yes!

REFERENCE LIST

Hendricks, G. (2010). *The big leap: Conquer your hidden fear and take life to the next level*. Harper One.

Understanding Your Reach

Learning Outcomes for This Chapter

After reading this chapter, you should be able to:

1. Determine how your leadership experiences can impact the education industry.
2. Effectively lead a transformational change project.
3. Learn how to connect your leadership experiences to innovative discoveries.

Questions to Reflect upon as You Read This Chapter

1. What transformational projects would you consider leading to impact change to the greater educational community?
2. What educational phenomena are you interested in researching?

One of the most impactful initiatives I had the privilege and honor of leading was the African American Parent Advisory Council. When I first decided to lead this transformation change project, I was simply responding to the concerns I learned about after listening to a few stories from African American parents and their children. These lived experiences led me to reflect on my childhood experiences in school and have a conversation

DOI: 10.4324/9781003325635-13

with my own daughter to learn about her perceptions and lived experiences in school. I discovered many parallels between generations, genders, and economic status for African American children in grades TK–12. I wanted to know how to change the narrative. I wanted to ensure that future generations would have new experiences and stories to share with their children. I wanted to empower the voices of a group of parents whose children disproportionately represented the highest student suspensions and the lowest college attendance rates. I took my concerns and preliminary findings to the superintendent of schools, and he fully supported and gave me the lead role to develop and implement a pilot AAPAC program which would later be adopted as a district-wide initiative. As you read the details of my transformational change project, please keep in mind it was implemented while I was still holding my primary function as a school site administrator. Leading with truth helps remind you of the limits and boundaries you were purposed to break. It's hard for me to imagine what would have occurred if I had ignored the stories of hurting parents to only focus on my job role. Do you know that you're more than a school principal? What ideas or projects are you currently overlooking? How do you use your strengths and assets to reach as many as you can possibly impact? Hopefully, you will be inspired to use your imagination and vision to lead change in your community, your district, or your school after reviewing the case study of my transformational change project.

▶ TRANSFORMATIONAL CHANGE PROJECT CASE STUDY

About the Project

The underperformance of African American students is attributed to historical inequalities in the educational system and poor economic conditions for African American families, which in turn cause a lack of parental involvement from African American parents. To solicit more involvement from African American parents, we must first identify how we want parents to be involved in the school system. According to Remillard (2005), parent involvement has multiple meanings. She asserts:

Their [parents] involvement tends to be classified along a "school centric" continuum. On this continuum, parents have "little power or influence over school decision-making process," and their "involvement" ranges from participating in extra-curricular, school sponsored activities to serving as classroom assistants or participating on a school council to, at the most extreme, serving as "partners in school problem solving."

(Remillard, 2005)

Research informs that minority parents who lack confidence and self-efficacy are less likely to become involved in the school setting. "The fact that minority and immigrant parents tend to have fewer resources and lower levels of self-efficacy and trust partly explains the parent involvement gap" (Shah, 2014). One way to build self-efficacy for minority parents is to provide forums for parents to understand the norms of the educational system. Shah (2014) points out that since the norms and values of the school system represent middle-class values and forms of communication, lower-income and minority parents may feel they are at a disadvantage and less capable to be involved. Understanding these and other unidentified variables can help schools establish meaningful relationships with various minority parent groups.

The African American Parent Advisory Council (AAPAC) is designed to equip parents and guardians dedicated to the success of African American children in the academic and social arena. With ongoing monthly meetings and continuous support, we provide necessary tools, information, and networking opportunities to help support parents in the success of their children. Similar to the English Language Advisory Council, AAPAC provides the school site council with tools and strategies geared towards improving culture awareness and diversity in the classrooms. Currently, AAPAC is offered at two schools in our district. The members of the African American Parent Advisory Council will work collaboratively to develop an implementation plan for district AAPAC groups. The goal of our committee is to continue the implementation process to ensure that each school has a well-established African American Parent Advisory Council. The transformational change project will focus on documenting practices and protocols that future AAPAC committees will be able to replicate at their school sites.

Transformational Leadership Team Roles

Resource Investigator. Significant in establishing relationships with community partners and parents. This role entails serving as a parent/community liaison between the team and the African American parents. This member is vital in distributing and collecting parent surveys, interviews, and student data. The mission is to make sure that parent and community voice is well represented in the decision-making process of the team.

Coordinator. Significant in facilitating meetings, delegating tasks, and moving the group forward. This role entails serving as the team leader and supporting all members as needed. This member is vital in keeping the group focused by using the team charter and team norms as guides to ensure effective participation and forward movement.

Monitor Evaluator. Significant in holding members accountable to their commitments. This role entails distributing consistent communication to remind members of meetings, deadlines, and budget updates. This member is vital in keeping structure within the team.

Implementer. Significant in showcasing the progress of the team. This role entails use of multimedia methods to communicate the accomplishments of the team to the public. This member is vital in establishing community buy-in and maintaining positive public relations about various events sponsored by the team.

Complete Finisher. Significant in polishing all team products before display. This role entails reviewing, editing, and revising all documents, flyers, and communication. This member is vital in being the master editor of the team.

Agreement and Team Commitment

In The Skilled Facilitator, *Schwarz (2002) defines the purpose of contracting as:*

> Clarifying expectations each of us has for the other: the objectives and boundaries of the facilitation, the ground rules for the group, issues of confidentiality, the roles of

the facilitator and group members, how decisions are to be made, and when the facilitation ends.

(Schwarz, p. 272)

Transparency is a foundational component to building effective relationships. The first meeting consisted of a four-hour session that entailed clarifying expectations through transparent discussions and team charter development. At the conclusion of the meeting, all parties were asked if they wished to continue team membership for the leadership project. All parties agreed to continue as a team member. The team charter was developed, and all members signed the charter as a symbol of their commitment to the leadership project.

Team Diversity

Sustainable change does not happen unless several levels of the system are touched and changed in a similar manner (McKee et al., 2008). To sustain the AAPAC parent groups at school sites in our district, our team has been developed with a diverse group of stakeholders. The stakeholder groups in our teams consist of (1) board of trustee, (1) assistant superintendent, (3) directors, (5) site administrators, (2) teachers, (2) parents, and (1) community representative. According to Birkman International (2009), organizations with effectively functioning multigenerational workforces have a strategic advantage. We consider our team possesses this advantage due to our multigenerational makeup of (5) baby boomers, (9) Generation X, and (1) Generation Y representatives. Drolet and Harvey (2006) assert in Building Teams, Building People "that as ethnic, cultural, and family diversity is expanding in the population at large, so too has the workforce become more diverse" (Drolet, p. 4). The dynamic of our team diversity will ensure that we have multilayered and multifaceted perspectives to ensure the success and sustainability of our project.

Effective Team Strategies

One of the most crucial team strategies we implement is effective communication. We believe it is imperative to communicate with honesty, integrity, and respect. We do not advocate for total agreement; however, we do value the tone, delivery, and intent of your communication. One of our norms is, assume good intentions. Our team has created a safe space to speak from the heart without malicious or ill intentions towards another team member. We have established a trusting and safe space for crucial conversations. Kegan and Lahey Laskow (2001) believe work relationships are damaged by perfectly delivered constructive feedback (Kegan, p. 128). We have identified the value of constructive criticism, and we embrace its relevance for making major decisions for district implementation plans. We conclude each meeting with a final statement from each team member to validate and confirm his or her position. We ask for honesty so that we fairly address misunderstandings and negative mindsets. Our goal is to continue to build a healthy and solid rapport with each other.

Vision, Mission, and Purpose

The mission of the African American Advisory Committee (AAAC) is multifaceted. We recognize that any positive endeavor will require the cooperation of all stakeholders: parents, schools, central office, and the community.

Parents. Encourage parents and teachers to work together to enhance the achievement and academic environment for African American students. Encourage and increase parental involvement by educating parents and students in the norms of the district. Become a vital part of the decision-making process in the education of African American students.

Schools. Develop cultural proficiency in teaching staff to address instructional and cultural needs of African American students.

Central Office. Recruit, train, and develop teachers, which better reflect the diversity of our student population. Be a visible and responsive entity to the needs of the responsible stakeholders of the African American community. Develop a strategic plan to increase parent education. This plan will concentrate on increased parent involvement, which greatly contributes to student success. The implementation and success of this plan will be monitored on an annual basis.

Community. Work in a collaborative fashion with members of the community (businesses, local churches, and municipal organizations) to develop strategies designed to empower the African American community.

African American Students Outcomes

I. An increase in the number and percentage of African American students who:
   a. Score proficient or advanced in reading and mathematics on state standardized tests.
   b. Successfully maintain academic letter grades of A, B, or C in upper-level mathematic courses (i.e., algebra, geometry).
   c. Are enrolled in Honors and/or Gifted and Talented Education (GATE) classes and successfully maintain academic letter grades of A, B, or C.
   d. Achieve an overall GPA of 2.0 (scale of 0–4) or higher in all academic areas.
   e. Enroll and complete two- or four-year college programs.
II. Decrease in the number and percentage of African American students who:
   a. Score Basic (B), Below Basic (BB), or Far Below Basic (FBB) in reading and mathematics.
   b. Have multiple suspensions or office discipline referrals.
   c. Are enrolled in special education for learning disabilities (excluding blind, deaf, etc.).
   d. Are referred to special education for learning/disabilities (excluding blind, deaf, etc.)

Team Cohesion and Team Focus

Our team norms are the foundational guidelines that drive our meetings, dialogue, and interactions. The norms were established in the second group meeting after the charter was established. The purpose of the charter was to establish commitment and purpose of the team. The purpose of the norms was to establish the behaviors that would drive us to upholding our commitments. We established our norms by first identifying the top five characteristics of an effective team. This process was conducted through a brainstorming process and group dialogue. Once we selected our top five characteristics of an effective team, we then identified actions that matched each character. We then rewrote our top five characteristics into action statements to establish our group norms. After reviewing the list of norms, each team member was asked to rate the norms in the categories of strengths and weakness. All members crumbled their list of weaknesses and placed them in a box. As a whole group, we reviewed the list of weaknesses and developed intervention strategies to assist with those areas of concerns. The whole group agreed to hold each other accountable to the consistent implementation of the intervention strategies. We believe that one weakness of the team member would greatly impact the growth of the group, and therefore, we assume the responsibility to help all members overcome their areas of improvement.

Decision-Making Process

Great teams make clear and timely decisions and move forward with complete buy-in from every member of the team, even those who voted against the decision (Lencioni, 2002, p. 207). One of the approaches we use in our decision-making process is the Workshop Method. Zuieback (2012) describes the Workshop Method as "'nominal group process' – meaning that conversation is minimized until the naming and reflection steps" (Zuieback, p. 78). This method involves five major steps: (1) setting the stage, (2) generating new ideas, (3) organizing, (4) discerning the consensus, and (5) reflection. After discussion, our team agrees to move forward with a decision collected from the data. This avoids bias, personal attack, avoidance, and neglect. The meetings conclude with all team members leaving the meeting and feeling as though their voice and ideas were considered and valued.

Accountability

An accountability atmosphere emphasizes that accountability is the inevitable partner of responsibility (Drolet, p. 191). One of the tools we use to maintain accountability is a project planner. The project planner is used for each major task or milestone related to our leadership project. For example, one of the barriers we identified with establishing AAPAC groups at school sites is the lack of trust between the African American community and our school district. In celebration of Black History Month, our team decided to host a Black History Month Gala to celebrate black heritage with our parents and community partners. In preparation for the event, our team used the project planner to assign tasks and monitor progress. Each meeting, the project planner was reviewed to determine if members completed their assignments. Additionally, the district approved and allocated funding to support the AAPAC coordinator positions at each site. The AAPAC coordinator will help facilitate AAPAC meetings, inform parents of pertinent events and activities at their sites, and provide their school site councils with budget recommendations from AAPAC members that are geared towards increasing student performance for African American learners. All sites are required to conduct a minimum of three AAPAC meetings for each school year.

▶ EDUPRENEURSHIP (EDUCATION + ENTREPRENEURSHIP)

For years I have taught students, parents, family members, and community members to "think outside the box." Lesson after lesson, presentation after presentation, and conversation after conversation, I have shared a list of inspiring leaders who've taken a leap of faith in their industries to completely transform it to something new. Yet I was failing to listen to my own message, and it was beginning to stifle my desire to stay in education. In Chapter 3 I talked about how the Truth Trek led me back to my core values. Once I rekindled a flame with me, myself, and I, the next step was to identify what I really wanted to do next with the skills, experiences, and passion I had for educating and mentoring others. I must admit, I felt stuck at first. I had the courage to do a new thing, but I still didn't know what the thing was for me to do. I decided to let it come to me naturally, and to my surprise, it didn't take long.

Motivation

It was February 2020, and two of my gal pals were invited to join my daughter and me for a Saturday movie night date. In the spirit of honoring girl power and black power, we decided to watch the movie *Harriet*, directed by Kasi Lemmons, starring lead actress Cynthia Erivo. The film is the biography of Harriet Tubman, an American abolitionist and social activist. Although I was familiar with the story of Harriet Tubman, the film was filled with so much inspiration. A major takeaway from the film was Harriet's selfless love for helping others. After escaping to the free North, she returned several times to help other slaves experience the freedom that was exposed to her. Watching her resonated with my spirit. I, too, wanted to help other leaders experience the freedom that I was beginning to enjoy after reconnecting to my core values. We didn't leave the parking lot before I shared with them my idea to establish an educational firm that would provide resources and support for school leaders. My gal pals enthusiastically encouraged me to get it started, and one of them asked, "What are you going to call it?" Before I could think long, the word *Minty* rolled off my tongue. It was the nickname Harriet's parents called her as a child before she legally changed her name to Harriet Tubman. On March 10, 2020, Minty Educational Services was birthed on the day that Ms. Tubman took her last breath and transcended to glory. Her legacy continues.

Say His Name

George Floyd. While excitedly working on the pieces of my new business, I watched the tragic devastation of a man gasping for air while being detained by law enforcement. My heart ached for many reasons, but I was especially moved by how much it impacted my daughter. She was a high school senior whose world had literally come crashing down. We were in the beginning of the pandemic, and it was the month of her 18th birthday. All our plans, surprises, dreams, and celebrations came to a screeching halt. We couldn't do anything but watch and listen to the world suffer. I believed what impacted her most were the social media posts she witnessed from those who lacked empathy for Floyd's death. She attended a diverse school and was friends with anyone and everyone who enjoyed her company, but the callous expressions she observed from certain peers made her question their friendship. We talked about her emotions at length, which gave me insight to feelings about her own identity she had been wrestling with for many years. Soon after, she decided to enroll in and attend a historically black university, and I decided that a pillar of my educational firm would be to educate school leaders on the value of creating diverse, equitable, and inclusive school communities. Just like Harriet led her community to freedom, my hope is to offer a safe space where leaders can examine issues of identity and equity as it relates to democracy and schooling. The intent is to offer my school leadership peers the liberty to challenge their thinking while exchanging stories in a nonthreatening atmosphere. So far, those who have participated in our DEI workshops have praised our facilitation and knowledge sharing. For me, these testaments are worth the sacrifice of my past. I have discovered, often, that tragedy leads to change. As for my daughter and me, our grief, empathy, and remembrance for a man who suffered for eight minutes and 46 seconds until he took his last breath are the catalyst that led us to action. I believe our actions will impact those we will have the honor of partnering with to lead our school reform efforts. His legacy continues.

Dynamite

My business development plans were making steady progress. With this new sense of purpose and direction, I decided to try something new. I applied for a higher education position as an adjunct professor for a summer course. Not just any course. Not just any university. I was focused. It was critical for every action to fall in line with my purpose. I looked for universities with mission and visions that aligned with my core values. And I looked to teach courses whose objectives involved theoretical principles that I was passionate about teaching to graduate-level students. Now remember, I mentioned earlier that it was important for me to let things happen naturally. One of my core values is to be carefree. Some people mistake careless with carefree. A careless person is someone who displays negligence. That's far from my

DNA. A carefree person, on the other hand, is someone who is free from anxiety. The new me was ready to stop worrying about everything all the time. Freeing up that worry space in my mind helped me to think creatively. What I didn't know was that my life was about to change forever. I was finally about to take a dose of my own think-outside-the-box medicine.

I was hired to work for a teacher preparation program whose philosophies of education greatly matched mine. Their course model is designed to have two instructors coteach the course. I did not pick my partner. He was assigned. Our section was added late, so we didn't have the same time as other partners to get to know each other and plan. We both were thrown in the trenches with less than a week to review the syllabus, required reading text, and design our summer course plan of study. This was out of my zone of comfort, but the new, carefree me was open for the challenge, and I was paired with a remarkably courageous partner to support my success. Since there was no time to waste, we set up two Zoom meetings to plan and design our curriculum. He was an experienced graduate school professor, and I was an experienced TK–12 school leader practitioner. We quickly discovered that we both were intellectually aligned and highly skilled pedagogy pros. It also helped that we shared similar community backgrounds. We were both roses who grew from concrete. Having a strong vibe helped balance our differences. My teaching style was more formal and structured, while his teaching style was more conversational and semistructured. It was a good fit, and students loved it. Together, we've now coinstructed hundreds of individuals who enjoy our hybrid teaching styles. People enjoy what makes him him, and they enjoy what makes me me. Together, we create dynamite!

For one of our last in-class activities, we divided students into five groups and assigned each group a chapter from one of our required readings. To be honest, neither of us were familiar with this required text, and given our short notice, we didn't have time to read it before the start of the course. Instead of instructing our students to participate in a traditional jigsaw, we instructed them to teach it to us as though we were middle or high school learners. The expectation was for all participants to lead one or more aspects of the lesson while we used a rubric to measure if they had incorporated the elements of culturally responsive and sustainable pedagogy we had discussed in class. Students were excited to present their lessons to us and their peers on the last day of class, and they were impressive. During one of the presentations, my partnered asked, "What if this was a competition show for teachers? Wouldn't that be fire?" I responded, "No, that would be dynamite!" Throughout the presentations, the two of us texted back and forth the elements of our make-believe show until it was time to give feedback and share our final sentiments with the class. The course was over, and the experience was life-changing. I was certain that I found my peace in higher education, where I would continue to teach and inspire future teachers and future school leaders. And just when I thought my time with my partner was over, I'd soon discover that it was only the beginning.

I received an email invitation from my summer course partner requesting to meet via Zoom on a Saturday morning. I accepted the invitation but did not have any idea what the meeting entailed. I just blindly logged on to see what he wanted to discuss. To my surprise, he provided a full business proposal on establishing a teacher competition game show called *BlackademX*. I vaguely remembered us discussing the name because we wanted to put a twist on the word *academics* since our goal was to highlight the successful academic and social connections between black teachers and black children. The concept was authentic, and the idea was enticing, but I couldn't imagine how I could juggle teaching, developing the firm, and cocreating a game show. Like, I had zero clues about the entertainment world. For my partner, no was not an option. He wouldn't even let me consider the idea. He mentioned a former colleague of his that he wanted to introduce me to for my consideration of a possible three-way partnership. It was so much to take in at once, but I must admit, I was excited about the concept. It was innovation at its best, where boxes and limitations were not welcomed. After our first official meeting in August 2020, the partnership was established, and the brand was legally registered. Our first BlackademX episode premiered in November 2020 and received hundreds of viewers. You see, folks, just like that, in less than six months, I owned two education-based, limited liability companies. My new title was, officially, edupreneur, and it has been the best experience of my entire career! Tag, you're it.

▶ JOURNAL ACTIVITY: NOTE TO SELF

Instructions: Think without limits. If funding and time were unlimited, what type of leadership project would you enact in your district or organizational network? How could you potentially transform it into a business?

REFERENCE LIST

Birkman International. (2009). *How do generational differences impact organizations and teams?* Birkman International.

BlackademX. (2020, November 8). *BlackademX: Financial literacy.* YouTube. https://youtu.be/X2J6kitwhaA

Drolet, B., & Harvey, T. R. (2006). *Building teams, building people.* Rowman & Littlefield Education.

Kegan, R., & Lahey Laskow, L. (2001). *How the way we talk can change the way we work.* Jossey-Bass.

Lencioni, P. (2002). *The five dysfunctions of a team.* Jossey-Bass.

McKee, A., Boyatzis, R. E., & Johnston, F. (2008). *Becoming a resonant leader: Develop your emotional intelligence: Renew your relationship: Sustain your effectiveness.* Harvard Business School Press.

Remillard, K. J. A. J. T. (2005). Rethinking parent involvement: African American mothers construct their roles in the mathematics education of their children. *School Community Journal, 15*(1), 51–73.

Schwarz, R. (2002). *The skilled facilitator.* Jossey Bass.

Shah, M. M. A. P. (2014). Linking the process and outcomes of parent involvement policy to the parent involvement gap. *Urban Education, 55*(5).

Zuieback, S. (2012). *Leadership practices for challenging times: Principles, skills, and processes that work.* D.G. Creative.

Final Thoughts: Author's Reflection

▶ **FINAL THOUGHTS**

Five years ago, you couldn't have paid me to think that I'd be writing this book. I feel like I've been constantly going since college. Once high school ended, life started, and it never slowed down. Somehow, I allowed the busyness of life to suffocate the dreams. After reading Langston Hughes's poem "Harlem," I begin to question at which point in our lives our dreams are altered. In the noun form, *Merriam-Webster* defines *dreams* as "visionary creations of the imagination." The etymology of *dream* derives from Old English and was defined as joy. Little children are blessed with the joy to creatively imagine "what they want to be when they grow up" and to think freely about reaching their goals and aspirations. Their freedom is based upon their limited experiences and lack of knowledge about the perceived truth of life. Over time, our daily routines and experiences help shape what we feel and believe is our truth. As we become older and encounter more experiences, our new truths become contrary to our dreams, which in the predicate form is defined as "a state of mind marked by abstraction or release from reality." From this perspective, dreams are inevitably deferred and quietly sit upon the bookshelves of our minds.

One of my truths is that I've always dreamed of writing books. I love writing. I love reading. I love telling stories. I love sharing aspects of my life to connect with others. I have used my craft of storytelling to connect with some of the most amazing students, teachers, staff members, families, and community members that I've been so honored to meet. For me, telling stories is how we connect. It's how we uplift each other. How we celebrate each other. How we forgive each other. How we empathize with each other. I believe power rests on our tongues. We have the power to advocate, the power to transform, the power to encourage, and the power to scorn simply by the words we speak, so use your words. It's time to dust those dreams off the bookshelves of hopelessness and walk in your purpose and in your truth.

At the end of my public speaking engagements, I typically lead the crowd in speaking a list of affirmations pertaining to the discussion topic I'm facilitating. In like fashion, I want to conclude this text by giving you permission to speak the truth you wish to see in your life, in your profession, in your school, in your family, in your community, in our nation, and in our world. What is your truth? Who do you still want to be when you grow up? Say these simple daily affirmations to cultivate your truths into beliefs, and watch your beliefs manifest into action!

ACTIVITY #10:
DAILY AFFIRMATIONS

- I am proud to be who I am.
- I am imperfect and perfectly me.
- I am allowed to be who I am.
- I deserve love.
- I deserve respect.
- I embrace the greatness within me.
- My mental health matters.
- My mind is full of brilliant ideas.
- I inhale confidence and exhale doubt.
- I am proud of who I am.
- I believe in myself.
- I am powerful.
- I light the world with my smile.
- My confidence is beautiful.
- I am brave.
- I will step out of my comfort zone and try new things.
- I am good enough.
- I release myself from anger.
- I choose my attitude.
- It's okay to start over.
- I trust myself.
- I will do my best with whatever comes my way.
- I am in charge of my future.
- Today is a new day.

- I am thankful for all that I have.
- I can make this a great day.
- I am special.
- I release fear from my mind.
- I learn from my mistakes.
- Nothing can steal my joy.
- I am designed for greatness.

Index

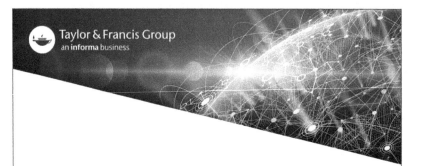